Living in Love
with Yourself

LIVING IN LOVE
With Yourself

by Barry A. Ellsworth

Breakthrough Publishing
469 Joye Street
Salt Lake City, UT
84107

© 1988 **Barry A. Ellsworth**

ISBN: 0-929175-00-X

Library of Congress Catalog Card Number 88-71331

Published by   **Breakthrough Publishing**
469 Joye Street
Salt Lake City, UT
84107

Copyright Acknowledgements

To Mindy,

without whose comings and goings in my life, this book would have never been written. And to all who read these pages, may they be a blessing in your lives.

Acknowledgements

I would like to acknowledge Leonard C. Hawes PH.D. and Marion McCardell for their assistance in the writing and editing of this book. I would also like to express my deep appreciation to Alan King and thank him for his support and friendship.

TABLE OF CONTENTS

	Preface	
1.	The Breakthrough	1
2.	The River.	5
3.	Addiction and Our Unconscious Beliefs	11
4.	Relationships.	23
5.	Rights in Relationships	34
6.	Creating Your Career	39
7.	Money	48
8.	Our Bodies of Spirit and Matter	54
9.	Sexuality	62
10.	Futuring and Pasting	73
11.	Conquering Your Fears	83
12.	Mastering Your Feelings.	94
13.	Using Your World as a Mirror	103
14.	Our Negative Ego	108
15.	Creating Intimacy With Yourself.	116
16.	Listening to Love.	120
17.	Developing Sensitivity	127
18.	Freedom	131
19.	Expressing Love for Yourself	138
20.	Accountability and Intention	145
21.	The Process of Creation.	157
22.	The Power of Commitment.	163
23.	Living from Your Vision.	170

Preface

Something is happening.....I see it.

All around me I'm noticing changes occurring in people's lives. I see shifts and movement in consciousness and spirit. Everywhere, I see transformation occurring.

A greater consciousness is emerging. An expanded, broader sense of self is bubbling up all over this planet and its source seems to be in the hearts and minds of men.

The tremendous technological advances of our day are evidence of this greater intelligence. In all parts of the earth I see men and women searching, asking, and finding answers to their problems. And the answer they are receiving seems to be the same; Love, Love of self, Love of others, and Love for the planet. Love, God, Goddess, All That Is, is coming to heal us, to teach us, to save us from our fears, our guilt, our false identities, our misguided desires, our hatred, and our anger.

I see it occurring for some, yet at the same time I see others struggling and in deep pain. I cry for them for I too have experienced pain. But I have learned that pain is one of Love's ways of healing and teaching us. And we have devised so many ways to avoid experiencing this pain. If we would only quit running from the pain and hurt long enough to learn the truths our suffering is attempting to share with us, our lives could be miraculously transformed.

This book is about Love and Truth...but it is also about pain and suffering. For Love sees and understands that if it takes pain to get our attention, Love will allow pain into our experience. If we would learn to listen to our pain, heartaches and suffering and hear what it is they are trying to tell us, Love could envelop us once and for all. And that elusive happiness and peace for which we have all been searching would at last be ours. "For man is that he might have joy."

THE BREAKTHROUGH

God is always with me.

I learn without resistance.

All I need shall be drawn unto me.

It was late June 1986. I had been at the home of a friend and business associate all night and well into the next morning. We had been having a discussion which I had carried on a hundred times or more in the past three years in one form or another with many different people. The topic was centered around how we were living our lives. What was it all about? We were both making six figure incomes and had seven figure financial statements. We financed business deals and made a killing. We drove some of the most expensive cars made, traveled throughout the world, kept company with gorgeous women, and dressed in the finest clothes money could buy. We also used huge amounts of cocaine and alcohol. And I was miserable. The alcohol and cocaine had helped to alleviate the pain in the early years, but they just weren't enough anymore. I wanted to know why my life was so unsatisfying and I wasn't finding any answers in the places I had been looking.

I had immense amounts of money and everything it could buy. A beautiful young woman was sitting at home waiting for me. Yet here I was having the same conversation I had had countless times before, and that old Rolling Stones' song kept going through my mind, "I Can't Get No Satisfaction". I was bored with myself, my life, and the conversation so I headed home. It was about 4:30 a. m. and no one was on the streets. I lived only a few blocks away, and as I paused at a stop light the answer came.

Suddenly it was as though a movie screen had been dropped in front of me about two or three feet away, and the movie being shown was my life in fast forward. There I was at a stop light on a cold, rainy night, watching every event of my life go before me. I was petrified. I had heard of people having such experiences as they were dying and I thought my time must have arrived. When the light changed I started driving, but the movie kept playing. My hands were glued to the steering wheel and sweat began to pour from my palms and forehead. My heart and mind were racing. I parked the car on the side of the road and continued to watch.

I was watching my life as a child, adolescent, and adult in three-dimensional, living color. The events were literally taking place right in front of me, yet I could still see everything else; my car, the road, the neighborhood and my body. Words can't describe what I was experiencing. I had no idea what was happening. I have never been so afraid and at the same time so amazed. As the scenes began to approach the present, I was suddenly aware of a voice speaking to me. I'm sure it was coming from within, but it was so intense it seemed to be outside of me. When it spoke it spoke to every cell of my being. What I heard went something like this:

"You just don't get it, do you? Your whole life is a lie. You really think that you are the stories you have made up to impress yourself and everybody else. You have no idea who you are. You think you are your car, your house, your money, your clothes, your drugs and your women. You think you own them. You believe you are your ideas, your thoughts, your concepts, and your con games. You think you are your illusions. And don't you see that's all they are? Illusions! Stories you tell about yourself because you have no idea what else to say. Dreams! Nightmares of your own making! And it's all been a lie! Who do you think is watching the movie?"

Then it was over. The projection was gone and so was the voice, but it seemed to echo from far away...it's all a lie! I felt drained and empty. What had just taken place? I was nervous, and extremely frightened. When I got home I tried to explain to my girlfriend what had just happened, but she was too angry at the lateness of my arrival, to listen. Thoughts of suicide were going through my head. Had this been meant to demonstrate that life had no real meaning? Or had I just missed its meaning? Did my life have any purpose? And what about the last line? It kept haunting me, "Who do you think is watching the movie?"

Since that cold, rainy morning I have looked for answers to that question, and I believe I have found some! This book is an attempt to share those I have found and continue to find.

THE RIVER

I let go knowing there is nothing to fear.

I am love.

My life is perfect.

I am perfect.

Let me share with you a paradigm, a way of viewing life which Love once shared with me at a time when I was experiencing pain. I have found it to be analogous to our lives in many ways.

Picture in your mind's eye a beautiful houseboat. You are on the houseboat floating down the most gorgeous river you can imagine. Everything is calm and serene. The water is crystal clear, having its origin in the mountain springs.

The water is teeming with all types of friendly, peaceful life, there for you to enjoy. You can see intricate formations under the water and beautifully colored fish and plant life. You might decide to drop anchor for a while and take a refreshing swim, or dip down and drink fully of the clean fresh water.

Along the banks there are fruit trees filled with mangos, oranges, avocados, grapes and figs. Everything necessary is there for you. The scene is absolutely gorgeous.

There are inlets and coves where you can stop and rest and experience all the delights of the shore. On the banks you meet other people. Some of these people seem interested in you. Others are going about their endeavors, not noticing you as you pass by. You feel calm and at peace within yourself. Everything is perfect.

After experiencing the wonders on this part of the river, you may feel an urge to continue down the river. You may invite others to join you. And you know that whatever they choose to do is perfect. You know the river has always shared with you the experiences that you have most needed for your personal growth and development.

This scene is a reminder to me of what life can be...peaceful, calm, tranquil, secure and friendly. This is what life is some of the time. But why not all of the time?

Floating down the river is easy. Everything you need is provided, if you surrender to the gentle promptings of the river's current. You experience what it offers and embrace it. The problems you create for yourself come about when you become attached to the people, objects, or experiences on the banks. Rather than continuing to float down this river of infinite Love and Knowledge, you choose to reach out and hang on to the experiences or objects on the banks. You begin to believe that you know more about what you need in your life with your finite knowledge than does the river of infinite Love and Knowledge; the Source of Life itself.

The objects are so pleasurable and beautiful that you want to possess them. It might be a wonderful moment in a relationship, a new Mercedes, and new job, or more money. The list of material possessions and emotional fantasies is endless. You become addicted to your emotional experience or to possessing objects. That's when the problems begin.

As you grab on to possess the desired object or experience, the boat comes to a tilting stop. You become the anchor. The current of the river begins to push hard against the boat. Or more accurately, you begin to fight against the naturalness of the river's current. The strain is tremendous. After a time, sand and debris in the river begin to lodge against the boat. As it accumulates, ever greater pressure is created and it becomes increasingly difficult to hold onto the objects. All the while you are becoming more and more frightened. You are afraid to let go for fear of losing what you are clutching. The pressure of the sand and silt steadily builds and your focus on the desired object becomes more and more intent. The tighter you hold on, the fewer choices you notice. Your strength and energy are being drained. Yet you continue to hold on.

If an observer on the bank were to pass by and see this, he could see the whole picture. And he would immediately see the solution. Let go! That's all there is to it. Let go.

This scene is analogous to how you create your realities. You can let go, surrender and flow, or fight with your fear of loss and your desire for some imagined identity. If you refuse to let go, eventually you will be pulled out of the boat.

You scurry about through life creating your careers, your relationships, your feelings, and your beliefs in this way. What you choose to focus on becomes the only thing that is real to you. In fact, you become the things upon which you focus your attention. If your focus is on the past, you are in the past. If your focus is on some imagined future, you are in that future. But when your focus is on the present, which in Truth is all that exists, you are flowing in this river of Love, Truth, and Infinite Knowledge. Can you change or influence the past in any way? Can you control the future--that which is yet to come? No. So why do you try so hard to do what you cannot? If you can learn to let go of your imagined identities, your belief systems, your thoughts, and learn to live in the Eternal Now, you will become much more sensitive to the currents of infinite Love in your life.

If you are reading, read. If you are listening to a friend, listen with compassion and understanding. Don't be thinking about what you are going to say next. If you are eating, enjoy the flavor and deliciousness of each bite and feel gratitude in your heart for the opportunity to nourish your body.

Have faith in the Love within you. Flow within its current. Why be afraid to let go? Haven't the gifts Love has given to you always been exactly what you needed? Isn't it true that your life has always been enough, if you allowed it to be?

So, let it all go! Let go of your thoughts and expectations about the way you think things should be. Let go of your past oriented guilt and your future oriented fears. Let go of your dreams, hopes, and imagined identities. Let go of the identity you have with the material possessions in your life. Let it all go, for anything you have to fight to hold onto is simply not yours. And as you let go you will probably find it was really not what you wanted anyway. Let Love create an infinite reality for you.

In the book, The Starseed Transmissions, Ken Carey eloquently writes,

> *"Perhaps you are concerned that some aspect of your identity will not survive the psychological process. You may be right. But you may just as well be wrong. Let it go. It makes absolutely no difference. There are no guarantees that this or that is going to survive the sight of God. But the only things that are threatened, the only things that will not survive, are things that do not exist apart from your conceptions, things that have no reality apart from the reality you give them.*

> *"All that is essential to you is being sustained by the creative power of the living God. All that you sustain in existence through the misuse of your creative abilities only serves to involve you in areas where your own life energies become mischanneled and eventually dissipated. Any belief, any concept, any conviction that you might have that truly mirrors what is present in the mind of God, will still be there on the other side of the psychological process. So have nothing to fear in releasing these things. All that has been sanctified by God will continue to exist. Only that which has sought to cheat you of your destiny will perish. It is really very simple; let it all go. See what the Lord has in store."*

Have faith in life. Trust in Love's love for you. Listen to what it is trying to teach you. Any hesitation is simply evidence that you are continuing to trust in fear and reason. Love whispers to your heart in many ways. Be attentive. Act on what Love tells you to do with your life. The joy that Love holds for you is immeasurable. Experience it!

ADDICTION AND OUR
UNCONSCIOUS BELIEFS

I forgive myself for thinking I have done

something wrong.

It is not a crime to be unconscious.

My experience has been perfect for me.

I forgive myself.

I love myself just as I am.

An addict is one who compulsively repeats certain behaviors. In modern society we tend to see addicts as "others" who take drugs or drink alcohol to extremes. Most of us never think it possible that we may be addicts. It's always the other guy. But may I suggest that we are all addicts. We are hard-core addicts in many ways, but we just don't see it and are afraid to look for fear of what we might discover. And what we are all addicted to is being right about our unconscious assumptions or beliefs, about the way we think things work in our lives and the world in which we live.

I have been an addict. Addiction doesn't work. And what doesn't work, doesn't work, no matter how hard we try to make it work. The paths I followed as an addict never brought about the desired results, but I refused to acknowledge the truth of my experience and continued to compulsively repeat what didn't work because it was familiar to me. I did what I knew how to do. I was an addict, and didn't see it.

One day Love brought a young woman into my life who gave me a wonderful book. The book was Handbook to Higher Consciousness, by Ken Keyes. In his book Keyes states,

> *"An addiction is a programming (or operating instruction to your bio computer) that triggers uncomfortable emotional responses and excites your consciousness if the world does not fit the programmed pattern in your mind. The identifying characteristic of an addiction is that if your desire is not fulfilled, you respond emotionally in a computer-like way and automatically play out a program of anger, worry, anxiety, jealousy, fear, etc. That which you emotionally avoid is just as much an addiction as is something you desire."*

> *He further states, "A practical rule of thumb for one starting on the road to higher consciousness is to grant oneself emotion-backed demands for physical necessities such as air; food, if starving, or shelter, if about to freeze-- all other addictions are sickness."*

With this understanding, which I now see and hold to be the truth of my experience, any time I become emotionally upset I know that I am confronting an addiction, meaning I am demanding that something be a certain way in my reality. And this demand is backed up with a great deal of emotion. When you become upset, a "red flag of warning" should immediately signal to you that you are working from an addictive pattern in your life.

A subtle difference that Keyes goes on to describe is the difference between <u>preference</u> and <u>addiction</u>. If you <u>prefer</u> that something be a certain way in your reality, your experience, and it isn't that way, <u>you do not become emotionally upset</u>. And that makes all the difference.

Handling your addictive behavior is a matter of relaxation. I am not saying that it doesn't take work, but the work is about learning to relax. If someone is late for an appointment, relax. It's okay. Your life will not be ruined. You may <u>prefer</u> that it be different, but it isn't, so just relax. If you find out your spouse is having an affair, relax. Your life is not going to end because of it. Relax! You do have a choice in the matter. You can go crazy and create all kinds of problems for yourself and others, or you can relax. It's up to you. You might prefer that it be another way, you might not like what is happening, but you don't need to destroy your peace and inner happiness over anything. Accept your experience. Embrace it. Become curious about your experience. Discover the truth of your experience. Then continue happily along your way. If you become aggravated, you are not <u>preferring</u>, but rather acting out an <u>addiction</u> by emotionally demanding your experience to be different from what it is. And this subtle difference between living in a <u>world of preference</u> as compared to living in a <u>world of addiction</u>, is the difference between Heaven and Hell.

The Cause of Unconsciousness

As human beings we have dual personalities. Our primary identity, who we are in truth, is our Spirit, or Higher Self. We are Eternal Beings of Light and Love. Our secondary identity is our physical body. Through our bodies we experience our worlds of sense, thought, and emotion. This secondary identity is most commonly referred to as our ego.

As each of us entered this material plane of existence and began to experience the gravitational effects of matter upon our consciousness, we each fell into deeper levels of unconsciousness and we began to experience ourselves as separate, isolated individuals. In doing this we began to identify almost completely with our bodies, our egos, our secondary identity. And it was through this process that our egos began to assume a function they were never meant to perform; i.e., <u>directing and guiding our lives</u>. Our negative egos actually deny the existence of the Spirit. Our negative egos are afraid that if they acknowledge the Spirit within each of us, they will cease to exist. The consequence of this has been an inner war. The Spirit, our Higher Self, attempts to guide and direct our lives, and the negative ego fights to do the same. The negative ego, in its fear, wants to be right about what it believes to be true. And our negative egos are very powerful.

As long as we continue to identify primarily with our bodies, our egos, we are going to have all kinds of problems. We will simply recreate our past experiences over and over again. We will run our programs. We will do what we know how to do, like any good addict. And all of us are addicts.

Beliefs and Assumptions

A belief is something we hold to be true. It is an assumption we make about the way we or the world works. When collected together, the beliefs each of us holds make up what I call our assumptive or belief matrix. A matrix is a mold or webbing. It is like a net. Our negative egos believe that without our assumptions and beliefs we would be lost. Our negative ego views our beliefs as a net that will catch us if we fall or misinterpret the world around us. If we are living our lives in accordance with beliefs that are true, meaning that they are accurate maps of the territory through which we are passing at any given moment, our lives work. We experience the results of our intention. But inaccurate beliefs and assumptions can become a ceiling or net that holds us into a confined area of limited possibilities. Our beliefs can actually deter us from reaching our highest potential and greatest good, if they are inaccurate maps of the way the Universe really works. And no matter how long or hard we persist at trying to do something that doesn't work, the results will be the same. What doesn't work, doesn't work.

Picture your inaccurate beliefs as a box which surrounds you. All you can see are the insides of the box. The box has become your prison. Unfortunately, the instructions on how to live a full and meaningful life are on the outside of the box. Until you can find a way out of the box, you're doomed to recreate your past. And there is no hope of escape. But there is a way out of the box.

Our Unconscious Programming

As a child growing up in a family of addicts, I developed many beliefs and assumptions about the world that simply don't work. At times the prices I have had to pay for holding on to these beliefs have been enormous. I have recreated the experiences of my childhood over and over again. And it hasn't always been a great deal of fun. Finding a way out of the box was difficult, but once I did, the opportunities to create anything I wanted became endless.

I am what modern-day therapists refer to as an Adult Child of an Alcoholic, an ACOA. My father was a severe alcoholic and my mother was the child of a very serious drinker, my grandfather. Thus my experience as a child was, to say the least, not always a healthy one.

My mother and father stayed together for fifteen years. Their relationship never grew or matured because of the alcohol, their addiction to inaccurate beliefs, and a refusal to change on either side. The marriage ended in divorce.

A book that helped me understand myself better, which I would recommend highly to any ACOA, is <u>Struggle for Intimacy</u> by Janet Geringer Woititz. Here she discusses in eloquent fashion many of the beliefs ACOA's hold to be true. I read this book shortly after breaking up with the woman I loved more dearly than anyone else in the world. It helped me work through the pain I was experiencing, and helped bring my unconscious, inaccurate beliefs about relationships to my conscious awareness. During this intense pain I felt deeply moved to write out on paper the experiences of my childhood. By doing that I was able to uncover the beliefs or programming that had been dominating and ruining my life; programming that I was completely unaware of. Once I understood that the maps or beliefs I had about relationships were inaccurate, I was able to begin a process of changing the way I assumed life to be and miracles began to occur. But I had recreated my parents' relationship twice in my own life before I began to look for answers to my problems. I was doomed to running my old programming. I created relationships that didn't work because I wanted to be right about my beliefs more than I wanted relationships that worked. Unconsciously I believed that I was unlovable, undeserving, unworthy, not really good enough to be loved, and that relationships ended in divorce. These beliefs were devastating to me. By being addicted to these unconscious beliefs, I recreated the very same situations I had experienced as a child; relationships filled with pain, arguing, conflict, anger, drugs and alcohol. And I thought I was just unlucky or with the wrong person. I had no idea that I had actually created the whole thing.

The first step I would recommend to anyone whose life isn't working out the way they had planned is to write down your childhood experiences. Put the whole of your experience, as you remember it to be, on paper then take a good look at your experience. The beliefs you formed as a child will become evident. This can be one of the most healing events of your life.

I found that all of the memories I had retained, the seemingly meaningless incidents, were not remembered by accident. My Higher Self, my Unconscious Self, had held on to them because these memories captured the moments when I developed, or began to develop my core beliefs. And my Higher Self knew that one day they would help me regain a state of wholeness--of spiritual, mental, emotional, and physical health and integration--so that I could some day create a world of Love.

As a child I experienced a great amount of anger, quarreling and violence. I was constantly being neglected. For years I blamed my parents for these seeming injustices, but Love has shown me that it simply wasn't their fault. They were doing the best they could at that time in their lives. They were doing what they knew how to do, what they had learned as children. And I have since come to see that none of their problems had anything to do with me. Yet I had believed for years that I was the cause of their problems. It simply never dawned on them or me that there were better ways to do things. Ways that worked.

My parents' personal problems were so immense that they never had much time for their children. So I developed beliefs that relationships and families were about rejection, abandonment and arguing. As far as I could see as a small child, family life had to have a lot of arguing in it, people abandoned one another emotionally and physically, couples had extra-marital affairs, and the father drank and smoked. It looked to me like whatever families fought about, the real issue was, "who was right." And no one conceded that he might be wrong--ever! And no matter what they had to endure they "gutted it out." Even if that meant fifteen years of physical and emotional abuse.

So I developed an assumptive matrix about relationships that simply would never work. In my adult life I unconsciously sought out others with whom I could act out what I knew how to do--engage in destructive, hurtful relationships which would eventually end in rejection, abandonment, and pain--because this is what I assumed relationships were all about. And like any good addict, I compulsively repeated what I knew how to do. But it never worked. And I had no idea that I alone was the cause of my problems in relationships.

As a child, I learned ways to draw attention to myself which seemed to work. I used to throw tantrums in fits of rage. I usually ended up being spanked or punished, but at least I was getting some sort of attention. From this I formed a belief that if I created enough turmoil, people would pay attention to me. I also learned that talking a lot got people's attention. And talking became a way for me to avoid pain. By constantly talking to myself and others, I didn't have to feel, and feeling for me was very uncomfortable because what I felt was usually a lot of pain, neglect, and hurt.

This "diarrhea of the mouth," has had detrimental effects in my life. Perhaps the most significant was that I never learned to listen, and without good listening skills one can never effectively understand others and thereby carry on meaningful communication. We have one mouth and two ears for a reason. Two thirds of our time should be spent listening and one third talking.

By observing my parents' behavior, I also developed a belief that I should try to convince others to see everything my way. I thought that convincing others would prove that my way was the right way, and would somehow validate my existence. So rather than learning to advise or share, I have always tried to convince, control, and manipulate others into accepting or adopting my way of thinking. And it doesn't work very well. But Love is sharing with me daily new ways to live my life and showing me beliefs and principles that work.

I have also had a difficult time defining boundaries. By that I mean defining where I end and others begin. Because I was physically abused, which is completely intolerable and unacceptable behavior in any situation, I had a very unclear sense of what appropriate behavior was. Was it all right to scream and yell at others? My experience said "yes," but that was an unhealthy context for living. And because of this I have had a difficult time allowing others to be who they are. It has been hard for me to allow others to be independent of me, to experience their own feelings and thoughts, to allow them the space to live their lives as they choose rather than how I think they should be living their lives. And many times I have thought other people were me. I assumed they felt what I felt, thought what I thought, and should do what I do. And I was sure I was right.

Love has taught me that <u>you can insist on being right, or have a relationship that works</u>, but you can't have both. And the addiction to being right about inaccurate beliefs will destroy any relationship.

Any addiction will eventually rob you of the joy Love is constantly offering you. Addictions might feel good for a while, but sooner or later they will diminish your long-term happiness.

Doing the Necessary Work

I once had a dream in which my addictions and unconscious beliefs were compared to an iceberg. The tip of the iceberg was all I could see and I kept chopping away at the ice until the iceberg was level with the ocean. At that point the iceberg would rise up and I became aware of a much greater portion of the whole thing. Once again I began chopping away at the ice until finally the iceberg was gone. I next saw myself lying comfortably on a beach basking in the warm sunlight. Everything in my life was wonderful. When I awoke it came to me that such work was necessary on a psychological level where my addictions and beliefs were concerned.

Observe what is taking place in your life. Ask yourself, <u>what kind of beliefs would a person have to have to create the reality you have created</u>. Be honest with yourself. Work with the problems, addictions and negative beliefs that come up for you. As you perform the necessary work of discovering your inappropriate beliefs and assumptions and releasing them you will become totally conscious of the addictions and beliefs which are causing any turmoil in your life. As your beliefs are discovered and appropriately dealt with, you can then choose to live by new beliefs that work, and life can become a marvelously fulfilling experience.

Many of us believe the bumper sticker that reads, "He who dies with the most toys, wins." We have become addicted to a belief which says one can find happiness through the accumulation of material possessions. In other words, "when the going gets tough, the unconscious go shopping." Experience has taught me that this is simply not true, but I spent millions of dollars trying to prove that it was. When my addictions and wants have become unbridled, there has never been enough to satisfy them. There was never enough money, love, sex, pleasure, or fulfillment.

Many such beliefs have been formed for us by the media. If someone from another country were to see our television advertisements for the first time, they would probably think that everyone in America was physically beautiful and drank beer in designer jeans every night of the week. It may be sick, and it may be an inaccurate portrayal, but it certainly influences us.

Due to such influences I developed a huge addiction to "pretty"! The girls I dated always had to be pretty on the outside. This addiction completely blinded me to what was on the inside. And it never dawned on me what needing to have a pretty girl with me, or an expensive new car or beautiful clothes was saying about me. As I began to embrace the reality of my experience, I realized that deep down inside I didn't feel very good about myself. I thought pretty things would make me pretty. Once I began to observe my experience it was obviously telling me that I held a belief that I was not pretty and that I was not enough by myself. And all the while I had been denying the truth of my experience. The results were a lot of unfulfilling, shallow relationships.

I was also addicted to pain. I know that sounds crazy, but I loved pain. My life was filled with pain, pain that I created because that was what was familiar to me. What would life be without it? Many of us have no idea, so we continue to create painful experiences because that is what we know how to do.

Another major addiction for me has been creating expectations about how life should be, rather than simply surrendering to what is and embracing my experience. I created expectations about my relationships and careers that simply were not true. They were illusions I had dreamed up from watching too many Cary Grant and Doris Day movies, along with "Leave it to Beaver" and "Ozzie and Harriet." And when reality didn't conform to my expectations I got mad! I have since learned to be very careful when it comes to creating expectations.

I have been addicted to resisting the principle that what I have is what I want, and what I want is what I have. For years I told myself that I really wanted something besides what I had, which of course destroyed the peace of mind and contentment I could have enjoyed by being happy with what I had in the present. This doesn't mean that we shouldn't set goals or strive to meet them. But our means should always be the same as our end. And aren't our goals always about making ourselves happy? So why not be happy while we're getting there? The decision to be happy is a simple one. Just be happy! That's all there is to it.

My list of addictions could go on for days. I used to get upset if my food wasn't prepared just right or if the light wasn't green when I pulled up to the intersection. Everything bothered me because I loved conflict and pain. I was addicted to people telling me the truth. I went absolutely crazy when my wife or girlfriend lied to me. I was addicted to people being on time. It was endless. I was as sick as they come, and I loved being sick. But if anyone tried to tell me I was sick, I got mad at them, like all good addicts do when somebody tries to take away their "stuff," meaning whatever it is they are addicted to.

What are some of your addictions? Does that question scare you? And are you addicted to being scared? If you begin to uncover your addictions and inaccurate beliefs and own that they are addictions, you will either have to change your behavior, or go to deeper levels of unconsciousness. You would have to work on yourself rather than making all of your problems somebody else's fault, which is what we all do at times.

Of course you don't have to look at your life or the results you have produced to this point in your life. You can choose not to. You can choose to stay in your prison, your box. And in your box, you will be doomed to recreate the past. You will get to experience more of what you have experienced in the past. And if you are completely satisfied with your experience of life, don't look. There's no need. If you are experiencing all of the joy, happiness and Love that you can handle, there is no need to search any further. But if you are reading this book, chances are that you attracted it into your reality for a reason. This book is probably about you. And the only way out of your problems is by working through them. Stand in the midst of your pain and problems and own them as the truth of your experience. Quit running from what Love is trying to share with you about yourself. I did for years, and the pain only got worse.

Maybe you are addicted to a fear of meaningful relationships because as a child you only knew about painful, broken relationships. So perhaps you overeat and no one is attracted to you. And no matter how many diets you go on, the weight won't come off. Look at the possibility that the weight isn't the problem, but rather the symptom of something much more subtle; your fear of commitment to meaningful relationships. And although you may not realize it, you love being afraid, because that is what you know how to be.

Maybe you're addicted to believing that you are really not lovable because you were always being rejected as a child by your parents or peers. And you are addicted to being right about this belief so you live life with a chip on your shoulder. You're "pissed off" at the whole world. And what do you get by being that? Well, you get to be right about your belief. You get to continue with your compulsive, addictive behavior and you get to experience a lot of loneliness and unhappiness. You are the creator of your reality. It's nobody else's fault. Do you want to continue to believe that you are unlovable, or would you like to create a new belief that says you are lovable and be loved? The choice is yours.

You can choose to discover who you really are and by doing so find new beliefs to live by, beliefs that work. I know in the beginning this can be one of the most painful things a human being can do, but what is on the outside of the box is beyond your wildest dreams. Trust me, staying in the box is much more painful.

Finding the Paradoxes

The first of the "Four Noble Truths" taught by Buddha was that "Life is suffering". Only when we understand this truth, can we transcend it. Only when we see that life is truly difficult will life cease being such a struggle. Life in its entirety is paradoxical by nature. Look for the paradoxes in your life--the different sides of the same coin. The answers to life's problems are available. You just won't find them by looking in familiar places. You've looked there for years and what have you found? They aren't found outside of you, but rather within. You create your outer reality from within. All the pertinent information needed to live a productive, satisfying, fulfilling life is available to you right now. It is within your grasp, but you, and you alone, are responsible for doing the asking. Only by searching your heart and your feelings, and by embracing the truth of your experience will you find the answers. This searching is not always easy. It takes effort but it works. Ask, and Love will help you every step of the way. And as you begin to uncover your addictions, remember to be gentle with yourself and love yourself just as you are.

Cease to identify so completely with your ego, your body. What you are first and foremost is Spirit. You are Love. You are an Eternal Being of Love, Light, and Truth. As you focus your attention on your Spirit, your Higher Self, and your negative ego begins to surrender to the Truth your Higher self shares with you, your life will begin to work in marvelous ways. Your Spirit was meant to direct your life. Your body and mind, your ego, were meant to be tools or servants to create a world of Love on this material plane, under the direction of your Higher Self. Love your ego, and as you do it will surrender to the Spirit. Learn to identify with your True Self, your Higher Self. Listen to what it is sharing with you. Then with your body act to bring about all that you can be; all that in truth you already are.

The world is filled with wonderful people and opportunities which can bring untold joy into our lives if we can learn to develop accurate assumptions and beliefs by listening to our Higher Selves. Daily we can attract new and exciting relationships and opportunities into our lives if we choose to.

Love is healing me. Love is healing the world. And Love wants to become a greater part of each of our lives. Love wants to teach us the Truth. Why resist the truth of your existence by continuing to trust in fear and guilt. What have the results of your life been to this point in time? Is your life really what you want it to be? It is possible to have all that you truly desire. Your life can work for you. That is the way it was meant to be. But you must first surrender to your Higher Self, to Love. Give up the belief that you, as ego, are all there is. Surrender to a life filled with and guided by Love. Let go. Trust in the Love within you. What have you got to lose? Let go and see what Love has in store for you.

RELATIONSHIPS

I am Lovable.

I am Enough.

I am Deserving.

I am Worthy.

I can have it All.

All of us are searching for intimacy, passion, companionship, and nurturing. Historically, we have looked for these needs outside of ourselves in the external world. But has it worked? The divorce rates in this country and the personal experience of many like myself are evidence of the fact that as a society we do not understand the basics of healthy relationships. Einstein once stated that, "The problems our world faces can never be solved by the same type of thinking that created them." And so it is with our relationships.

The Price of Denial

Intimate relationships had always been very difficult for me because I tried to structure them according to the belief systems, or programming, I had formed as a child. In many areas of my life I believed that by myself I was not enough. So I created a huge image of who I thought I should be, with money and all that it could buy, to compensate for this belief. Understand, however, that I was completely unconscious of the belief I held that I was not enough or was unlovable. If someone had told me that I didn't love myself or lacked self respect, I would have laughed at them. I have now learned to listen more intently to the messages the Universe shares with me. My old outdated maps of relationships simply didn't work, just as they hadn't worked for my parents in my childhood. But not being conscious of my belief systems at the time, I did the only thing I knew how to do. As any good addict does, I went about recreating my childhood experiences. When my marriage and other relationships ended, I beat myself up for having failed. I quickly found ways to avoid my pain with drugs, alcohol, or sex and started off again trying to fulfill my inner needs outside of myself. But the Universe always serves up the same lesson over and over again until we learn it.

I was endlessly putting the cart before the horse in my relationships and recreating the nightmare of my childhood; another relationship that didn't work. I never took the time to get to know the women I went out with or to develop any type of intimacy with them before I got into bed with them. I thought sex was intimacy. I now see that premature sexual relations actually blocked my ability to create intimacy with the women I was involved with by blinding me to who and what they were really like as individuals.

I attracted women to me with money, fancy cars, big houses, alcohol, or drugs. If I didn't have sex with them early on, I lost interest. And, paradoxically, I usually lost interest even if I did. Three years after my divorce I met a young woman with whom I recreated my marriage. The similarities were frightening. Both she and my ex-wife were twenty years of age when we met. Each of them had developed ulcers at the age of seventeen, by repressing their emotions and refusing to communicate their real feelings. Both were modeling to make a living, and very image conscious. They both had tremendous difficulty accepting and loving themselves as they were. They believed that lying to others about the truth of their emotional experience and what they were doing with their lives really worked. They thought that their lies would somehow cure or do away with their feelings of insecurity, inferiority, and lack of self love. Most of the arguments we had were about telling the truth but in each case they were convinced that I was mad at what they had done rather than the lying. In fact on any given day you could take anything either of them said, divide it by their social security numbers and still have grave doubts about finding any truth in even the remainder. And these were the women I had attracted to me. When I broke up with this girl she moved into an apartment, in a city of considerable size, which was only three doors away from where my ex-wife had moved after we parted company. A short time later we took a trip to Mexico, just as I had done with my ex-wife. I knew then that there was more to what was taking place than mere coincidence.

When this relationship ended, the pain was excruciating, but for the first time in my life I stood in my pain and embraced it. And by allowing myself to experience the pain, the walls of my prison began to dissolve.

I now understand what Carl Jung meant when he said that, "neurosis is the natural by-product of pain avoidance." I had devised so many ways to avoid pain in my life that I had created a reservoir of emotional pain desperately seeking an outlet. Allowing myself to experience my pain was the very thing that began to heal my mental illness-and I was sick. It still amazes me that the pain I had been running from my entire life turned out to be my savior. Experience the pain in your life. Love uses pain to teach you how to do what works. Pain can heal you if you allow it to run its course. Love your pain. Embrace your pain and ask it questions. Go within yourself and ask what the pain is about and what it is trying to share with you. The results can be miraculous. Let me share with you some lessons pain has taught me.

Falling in Love

Falling in love is a paradox. On one hand "falling in love" is perhaps the biggest lie ever made up about love. What our society refers to as "falling in love" is in part a breakdown of our ego boundaries. I like to call it an emotional orgasm, or a substitute for the true spiritual experiences for which we are all searching. Yet like all experience, it is paradoxical. I don't believe we would have the courage to enter into relationships and engage in the growing process relationships provide without this initial breakdown of our ego selves and the feeling of oneness the act of "falling in love" provides. But when the "honeymoon" is over, you will fall out of love. The boundaries of your ego self will eventually snap back into place and the oneness will cease. It is at this point when deep, meaningful relationships can begin and real love develop, or a parting of the ways will occur.

The Sins of the Parents

As a child, I normalized many behavioral patterns which were not conducive to healthy relationships. From watching my parents' behavior I learned to act like they did. And I was programming my mind to recreate similar situations. For example, I have always tried to control the actions and beliefs of others, just as my parents had done. It didn't work for my parents and it hasn't worked for me either. And for many years I wasn't even aware of what I was doing. I was a control junkie. But I was too deep in the forest to notice the trees.

Because my parents had stayed in their destructive relationship for years, I learned to be loyal at any cost. I developed tunnel vision where relationships were concerned. No matter how destructive a relationship was, I was committed to it. Most of my relationships have been full of sound and fury, but not a great deal of joy and wonderment or spiritual and emotional growth. I have learned they can be.

As a child I learned to drink, smoke and take drugs, all of which don't do much to promote healthy relationships. I thought, "This is what a man does." I also learned to argue and scream a lot. That's what I thought normal relationships were like. And until I was able to bring these source relationships with my parents to completion, I went through life recreating their relationship in my life. I was creating destructive relationships filled with conflict. Then I met this young woman who assisted me in coming to a greater awareness of how I had been living my life. Her name was Erin.

Nightmares or Blessings

When we first met, it felt like magic. I gave her my best song and dance. I told her she would never have to work again and that I would buy her anything she desired. And she believed me. However, both statements were entirely contrary to how I really felt about relationships, but instinctively I knew that was what she wanted to hear. Physically, she was one of the most attractive women I had ever seen. And being the junkie I was, I was sure I had found the perfect "fix".

When we met, she identified almost completely with her body. She thought she was her body, as I thought I was mine. Her greatest concern in life was how she looked and dressed. As I came to know her better I realized that she had one of the most brilliant, perceptive minds I have ever encountered. But she found absolutely no satisfaction in any type of intellectual interaction or stimulation. If it wasn't in "Vogue" or "Cosmopolitan", it didn't interest her. We both had very addictive personalities and similar beliefs concerning money, pretty, and sex. And we were both looking for that perfect person to make our lives complete. I had plenty of money and she was the prettiest thing I had ever seen. I took her to Mexico for two weeks and spent thousands of dollars to impress her. She loved it. A week later she moved in with me and the fun began. She often said she wanted to marry me and have children. I told her that she was very young and was going to grow and change a great deal. I said I would marry her in a few years if she still wanted me to. What I was unconsciously saying was, give me some time to prove to you that I am unlovable and that I don't deserve to have this relationship. And I did. Most of the time I treated her like gold, but all too frequently I patronized her, flirted with other women, and belittled her in front of friends and family. She chose to stay and we both got exactly what we wanted. We both got to be right about our unconscious beliefs that we were unlovable and undeserving. During this period I quit using drugs, began writing, and became involved in experiential trainings. Erin felt very threatened by all of this.

At the end of a year and a half the perfect relationship we had both envisioned was a shambles. I was forty pounds overweight and near bankruptcy. I had lost more than a quarter of a million dollars in a business venture I had entered at Erin's urging and had blown the rest on drugs, parties and vacations. I had no idea what I wanted to do with my life so I began to focus my entire life on her and her career as a model and singer. The only problem was that she didn't want to work at either of them. She was very lazy, and wanted someone to take care of her. I despised her laziness, but continued to put up with it. As time went on we were arguing constantly about everything. We were two passive co-dependent junkies waiting for each other to make our lives work.

As a child Erin had learned to argue with her father. She was a gifted athlete, but when she lost interest in athletics, her father lost interest in her, and the fighting began. She started doing everything possible to hurt him by rebelling against his religious beliefs. She once told me that when she was a teenager her father refused to talk to her for 3 months because he was angry at her. How painful that must have been. She also hated her grandfather passionately. He was mean, drank, and had affairs with other women. He kicked Erin out of his house one time for not washing his dishes to his expectations and told her never to come back. After learning of this I understood more fully why Erin despised cooking and cleaning. Erin's grandmother contracted syphilis from him and eventually died from it. Her grandmother was the joy of Erin's life and her death and its cause were a terrible blow. It's not hard to understand why Erin developed some less than healthy beliefs concerning men.

When I was a young boy my mother used to scream at me and physically abuse me. I formed a belief in those early years that women were out to hurt me and that they didn't love me. I didn't realize that the anger my mother expressed towards me was really anger meant for my father and her father. I thought she was angry at me. So I began to punish her with all types of rebellious behavior and unconsciously decided that I was going to hurt women before they hurt me. But the person I ended up hurting most was myself. The sword I wielded cut both ways. And Erin held similar beliefs about men. <u>We were perfect mirrors for one another</u>. We were unconsciously doing everything possible to prove that we were right about our beliefs that we were unlovable and that relationships ended in rejection. We were both unconsciously self-destructing in the relationship. We were both recreating the experiences of our youth.

Gandhi taught that, "A thing can be retained by the same means by which it has been acquired." One evening she was out at a bar with her friends and met a male dancer who was quite attractive. Four days after meeting him she said she was going to move out, and I said "fine." When the money, the excitement, the good times, and my self-confidence were gone, she was gone!

Two weeks later she was in Los Angeles with her new found friend and the pain of withdrawal engulfed me. I have never in my life experienced such bitter suffering. But for the first time I faced it. I had come to realize that all of the ways I had depended on to avoid pain didn't work. I was no longer drinking or taking drugs. This time I was going to try something different. I was determined to face the pain and discover how and why I had created the same experience twice in my adult life. And Love began to heal me through this immense pain. This is when I felt deeply impressed to write about my childhood, and as I did all of my unconscious, inappropriate beliefs concerning relationships began to surface. One by one I came to understand them and was eventually able to let them go. But it was a difficult and effortful task.

A short time later Erin became extremely ill and came back to live with me. And not realizing the extent of my addiction, I allowed her to move in. I wanted to share what I had learned with her and put our relationship back together on a more sure foundation, but she refused to listen to what I had discovered about myself. She was still sure that the answers to her problems were going to be solved with money, a glamourous life, and another man. Two months later she moved into her own apartment, and within a few weeks the relationship was over.

It was then that Love began to teach me new ways of living my life. Love began to show me how to open my heart in a very dramatic way to hear the messages and truths It had been attempting to share with me. Love brought a wonderful book into my life entitled <u>Living in the Light</u> by Shakti Gawain. In this book she gives a very clear explanation of the male and female energy in each of us:

> *I think of our female aspect as being our intuitive self. This is the deepest, wisest part of ourselves. This is the feminine energy, for men and women. It is the receptive aspect, the open door through which the higher intelligence of the universe can flow, the receiving end of the channel. Our female communicates to us through intuition--those inner promptings, gut feelings, or images that come from a deep place within us. If we don't pay conscious attention to her in our waking life, she attempts to reach us through our dreams, our emotions, and our physical body. She is the source of higher wisdom within us, and if we learn to listen carefully to her, moment by moment, she will guide us perfectly.*

> *The male aspect is action--our ability to do things in the physical world--to think, to speak, to move our bodies. Again, whether you are a man or a woman, your masculine energy is your ability to act. It is the outflowing end of the channel. The feminine receives the universal creative energy and the masculine expresses it in the world through action; thus we have the creative process.*

> *Our female is inspired by a creative impulse and communicates it to us through a feeling, and our male acts on it by speaking, moving, or doing whatever is appropriate.*

I have learned that if one is to ever have healthy relationships in the external world, one must have a healthy relationship with oneself internally. Our outer world is simply a reflection of our inner world. The real purpose of the relationships and situations we attract into our lives is to teach us about ourselves. They aren't there by coincidence. We actually create them. We attract them into our lives to show us where we need to work on ourselves.

Another look at "Falling in Love"

Let's look at another side to the act of "falling in love." This feeling of "falling in love" is the Love of the Universe flowing through us and our own inner beauty and talents are being mirrored by or projected onto another person. Relationships with other people serve a very important function as mirrors. If you are male, you project your inner female. If you are female, you project your inner male. Our Unconscious Mind, or Higher Self, knows who would best enhance our growth at different points in our lives. And that's why we "fall in love." You are projecting your contrasexual archetype onto another person to assist you in becoming more aware of who you are in your entirety.

In a healthy relationship, one's focus should always be on one's self. You can never be committed to another person unless you are first one hundred percent committed to yourself and making your life work. Anything you see as a fault or weakness in another person is your weakness, just as any positive attribute or quality you perceive is also a part of you. It is impossible to perceive something in someone else unless it exists within you. And when you find a trait in your personality that needs work you're the one that gets to do the work and grow. You don't get to vote on what others choose to do with their lives. Work on your self. This perhaps might sound selfish, but it is the only thing that works. As Shakespeare said, "This above all: Unto thine own self be true, and it must follow, as the night the day, thou cans't not then be false to any man."

Getting Clear

We have chosen to live in this world of matter. If we are ever going to have healthy, loving relationships with others, we must first learn to have healthy, loving relationships with ourselves. To do this we must learn to integrate the female and male energies within each of us. We must learn to seek the direction of our Higher Self, then act on that direction. Be the right person. There is then no need to look for the right person. When the student is ready, the teacher will appear. And get clear about your intention. What do you want from a relationship? Here are three suggestions. First, make sure you are both physically attracted to one another enough to hold the relationship together. Looks are certainly not the most important thing in life, but they are important. Second, make sure that you are both on the same intellectual levels. If you don't understand one another intellectually, the relationship is going to be very difficult for both parties. And third, make sure that you are both headed in the same direction, meaning that you want the same things out of life.

Once you are clear about your intention, it is then simply matter of attraction. As we work on becoming whole and integrated within, as we learn to love ourselves completely, the loving, nurturing people we desire will come into our lives. Much of this inner work has to do with honestly acknowledging our feelings, desires, and experience, owning where we are at this point in our lives, and then sharing the truth of our experience with ourselves and others. It takes time and patience as we work on our inner selves, but all we need for our personal growth and development will be drawn to us when the time is right. It's that simple!

Trust the Process. Stay in the Process.

As we come to understand and accept this, we will begin to see that all of our relationships are perfect for our growth into higher consciousness. The purpose of life is to come to a total, conscious awareness of who we really are. We are here to learn about feelings and emotions, thoughts and form, matter and spirit, and what healthy relationships between these things are. Whatever it takes to bring us to consciousness is what it takes. As the Consciousness, the Love, the Truth within us begin to magnify and grow, as we learn to channel more Love and share it with those around us, our field of loving influence grows. And the process of learning becomes less and less painful. The Love and Light in our lives becomes ever greater. People will be naturally attracted to our Love and will want to share our Love and understanding of life. For in truth, how well we understand the world depends on how much we love the world and the life forms in it. When we experience pain or anxiety and repress it, rather than owning and embracing it with our Love, we begin to experience confusion in our world of feelings, thoughts, and emotions. But as we allow Love to flow within us and through us, it cleanses us. It clears away the emotional blockages like water flowing through corroded pipes. At first it may be only a few drops, a trickle, but as time passes, the water begins to wash away the corrosion until it gushes freely through the open, cleansed pipeline. Our understanding and our capacity to love then become much greater.

Once this flow of Love begins you become more attuned to your deeper feelings and intuition. You no longer react to situations based on your old belief systems, but rather act spontaneously in the more appropriate ways that Love shares with you in the moment. As your own inner female and male energies begin to interact in a healthy way, you begin to find yourself becoming less and less dependent on other people to fulfill your needs.

At times this process of drawing back into yourself to do the necessary work within may feel very uncomfortable and frightening to the people in your life, and to you. But as you become more integrated and whole within, the people with whom you are sharing your life will begin to grow as the increase of Love begins to flow outwardly from you. Or they may resist and choose not to grow and leave the relationship. They may find it very uncomfortable experiencing more Love and Truth in their lives and choose instead a continuing relationship with fear. This does not mean that they are bad people. It simply means that they are where they are in their lives. They might not be ready to progress as quickly as you. Or they may have other issues to deal with. Allow them to be where they are. Love them enough to let them go and grow. And whatever happens, know that it is perfect for your growth and development. You are on a journey of becoming all that you were meant to be. Embrace the journey. Trust the process.

RIGHTS IN RELATIONSHIPS

To love is to let go.

To let go is to grow.

Holding on stops the vibration.

Holding on inhibits growth.

Every success is a failure.

Every failure is a success.

People in relationships have certain rights that should never be violated. And with each right comes an accompanying responsibility.

The Right to Privacy

First, you have the right to privacy, the right to your own space to be all of who you are, and to be alone with your deepest thoughts and feelings. You need moments, spaces in time, to be by yourself, to connect with your feelings and find your sense of direction. And in a relationship, this right of privacy should never be used inappropriately. Spending time alone should not be done impulsively or in ways that would make others worry unnecessarily. All of us need our own space to heal and be nurtured from within. Allowing yourself such privacy and space to be alone, and allowing others the same right, is essential for the growth and stability of a productive, healthy, loving relationship.

The Right to Grow

You have the right to grow. No two people grow in the same way or at the same pace. And if the freedom to grow is not allowed, any relationship is doomed. Placing restrictions on other people or hindering their right to grow in any way they see to be in their own best interest simply doesn't work. People in relationship should compliment and support one another so that both can reach their fullest potential and become all of who and what they were meant to become. A relationship based on this principle can only become enriched. Partners in such a relationship will stay together because they choose to, not because they have to. They want to be together, not because they need to be together or because of some promise they made in the past, that no longer lives for them but because they enjoy being together and experience growth in the relationship. In such an environment both lives flourish and unfold in beautiful, dynamic ways.

The Right to be Trusted

You have the right to be trusted. And with that right comes the responsibility of being worthy of such trust. Your thoughts and words have a right to be heard, respected, and trusted as an expression of the truth of your experience. In this type of relationship, both are equals and together the whole is greater than the individual parts. You have the right to be trusted until you have given others sufficient reasons to believe you are not worthy of such trust. Trust is a fragile thing that is easily broken. Be sensitive of your words and actions so you don't send double messages. An example of a double message is screaming out, "Yes, I love you. How many times do I need to say it?" Which message should you believe, the words or the anger? Until you learn to integrate your non-verbal messages with your verbal so that a cohesive message is being sent, you can be sure the question will come up again. But if both parties are conscious of their words and actions, the trust and love between their souls will grow and mature.

Be aware of situations which could raise doubts or fears in your companion. By living from these principles, trust and mutual respect will increase. Individual integrity will blossom. The bonds of Love between you will strengthen. And the Love between you will flow as the waters of a deep and powerful river, and no matter where you go, as seperate individuals, you will never be alone. For you will know and feel the love and trust ever flowing between your spirits. Who in their wildest dreams would walk away from such a relationship?

The Right to Defend Yourself

You have the right to defend yourself and to defend your rights. If you do not defend yourself, who will? If you are constantly being used or taken advantage of in a relationship, don't allow it. Never give your power as an individual to another. By doing so you simply weaken yourself and decrease your ability to function in appropriate, healthy ways. Stand up for your rights as you allow others to exercise theirs.

The Right to be Respected

You have the right to be respected. Your beliefs, thoughts, feelings and opinions have the right to be expressed and heard and given as much importance as another's. Your rights as a human being should be respected. And if one chooses to grow apart from another and end a relationship physically, that right should be respected also. You have your own life to lead and you alone are accountable for your life. You are free to choose whatever you see to be in your own best interest. And the right to choose your own path should be respected even when it might be painful. You don't get to vote about how others choose to live their lives. You only get to vote on yours. If your rights are not being respected or you are not respecting the rights of others and your relationship comes to an end, know that it is only a separation of your bodies. For once a bond of Love has been created, in your hearts and minds you will always be together. And with the passing of time the wisdom of all things shall be made manifest in your life.

The Right to Seek Your Own Happiness

You have the right to seek your own happiness in any way you choose. This does not mean that you should run around seeking happiness without taking the feelings of others into consideration, but sometimes your happiness is not another's, and you choose to say goodbye.

The Right to be Accepted

You have the right to be accepted just as you are, and loved for what you can become. Accepting a person's weaknesses is as important as accepting their strengths. Your job is to love as best you can and accept and embrace yourself and others as a process, rather than a product. To love is effortful. To love is to be in the service of others. Sometimes accepting another just as they are is difficult, but great growth can occur by doing so.

The Right to Friendship

You have the right to have other friendships and interests. One person cannot supply all of your needs all of the time. This does not mean that your commitment to a relationship should be set aside. In a relationship of commitment and trust both parties have no need to fear outside influences; they should embrace them and rejoice in the growth they offer. And it is commitment that makes the difference between productive relationships and fearful ones. Commitment allows for privacy, space, trust, and other healthy friendships and interests. Without such commitment relationships can become very painful and scary. Never use this right inappropriately or as a weapon against one another. Love one another and grow together.

The Right to be Loved

You have the right to be loved, and the right to share your love with another. Without Love life is meaningless. To love is to share, to be intimate, to be listened to and understood, even when we may disagree. And I have seen time and time again that there is no real disagreement when Love and Truth are present. Disagreements occur only when you are reacting out of fear and the illusions its shadow casts upon you. Love others for who they are and what they can become. And accept no less from anyone else where your own needs for love are concerned. Remember, Love is gentle and kind. It is patient and caring. And when shared between two people, it can develop a bond, a kinship, an understanding that words cannot describe, nor time and space erase. It is something that can only be felt in our heart of hearts. Learn to be gentle in the special relationships that Love has offered you to enrich your life. Be kind to those sacred companions who have chosen to share their lives with you. Be ever thankful for the Love those closest to you have chosen to offer. Cherish it always.

I believe by nature all human beings are good, and all are on a journey of discovery which will eventually take them higher. But in our travels let's choose to make our journeys and the journeys of others as pleasant as possible. I know that without pain there could be no joy, but I think we could all do a better job of reducing the pain we offer others.

CREATING YOUR CAREER

My life does have purpose.

I do have a part to play.

I am always guided to my highest good.

By loving myself I become a blessing

in the lives of others.

I do have impact.

Work is something I have come to hold as a great blessing. What would life be like if you had absolutely nothing to do? There have been times when I didn't have to work for the necessities of life, and I have learned that I can become very bored and depressed if I am not engaged in a some type of productive, creative endeavor. And work becomes play, when you love your work.

I have done many things in my life. I am living proof that you can be anything you want to be. I have been a musician, a jockey, a missionary and a car salesman. I've attended college and law school. I've been a stockbroker, business consultant, venture capitalist, night club owner, lecturer and author. I have been a millionaire and bankrupt. And I have learned great lessons through it all; lessons about dedication, hard work, money, laziness, failure and doing things for the wrong reasons. But the most important lesson I have learned is that <u>if you don't love what you are doing to make a living, don't do it</u>. Boredom is the soul's way of telling you that you have learned all you can in a particular situation.

Statistics show that eighty percent of the work force in the United States doesn't enjoy what it is doing to make a living. This is pathetic. If human beings are spending half of their waking lives performing a task simply to make money, and that task by itself brings them absolutely no satisfaction or fulfillment, what is the quality of the rest of their lives going to be like? In America drug and alcohol problems, spousal and child abuse and violent crime are rampant. I believe this indicates in part that dissatisfaction with our work spills over into the rest of our lives. Who would marry someone they don't love? In essence, that is exactly what you are doing when you become involved in a career you don't love and that is not satisfying or fulfilling to you. There is a marriage between you and your career, like it or not. In fact, two of life's most important decisions are those you make about your career and your relationships. These two areas will have a greater impact on your life than anything else, because the majority of your life is spent in relationship to your chosen career and in relationship to the people closest to you.

Owning Who You Are

By nature I teach. As a car salesman all I wanted to do was teach people how to buy cars intelligently and teach other salesmen how to sell. As a stockbroker I taught my clients about the markets and other brokers how to become better brokers. But I continually self-destructed in my careers, and didn't begin to understand why until my breakthrough at the traffic light.

I had been living a lie. I wasn't a car salesman, broker, or venture capitalist by nature. I was a teacher, but I was afraid that I wasn't good enough to be a teacher. I didn't think that I had the proper education or the credibility or enough experience in a given area or enough money or that I really had anything to say. And until I embraced the truth that I was meant to be a teacher, I continued to self-destruct.

The truth of your existence can be found out by engaging in an inner dialogue between your ego and your Higher Self, or Love and by observing the results in your life. This dialogue and observation can take place voluntarily, or painfully. Pain comes during crisis. And if you are constantly going against the direction of your Higher Self, you will create crisis situations in your life. This type of pain can knock you to your knees. You can then engage in this inner dialogue and observation or again choose not to, and experience more pain until you get it. And you will eventually get it. In this lifetime or ten thousand lifetimes later. Love is not going to give up on you. Don't give up on yourself.

I believe that everyone on the face of this planet has a specific task or tasks to fulfill; a mission to accomplish. Each of us, with our unique and special talents has a contribution that only we can make to the world. I believe this with all my heart. Love has shown the truth of it to me.

This does not mean that all of us were meant to be presidents of vast corporations or financial wizards. It does mean that each of us has our own special gifts and talents. If you will search your feelings and be attentive, letting go of all your preconceived notions about the way things are or should be and listen to your feelings, your heart, Love will reveal to you what your special talents are. You will find that these special talents or gifts are really what you have always wanted to do all along. And you will find that you are probably very good at doing what you love to do most.

When I was younger, there were three things I loved doing--playing music, riding race horses, and teaching. Yet, when it came time to make a choice about my career, I focused on law school because I thought it would bring me money and prestige. Law was something I thought my context, my environment, would approve of, and I assumed that the source of my satisfaction was going to come from outside myself. I never seriously considered the possibility of music, horses or teaching as careers. And what I found by going outside of myself for answers was not very satisfying in many ways. I became involved in careers that at times produced a great deal of money, but also some less than desirable side effects like boredom, drugs and alcohol abuse, and divorce. And it was perfect for my growth and development. Love has since taught me the importance of being who I am and loving myself as I am. The blessings this has brought to my life and those around me have been immense. I have a vision, as crazy as it may sound, that everyone on this planet could be engaged in a labor of Love, and everything would work out just fine.

Shifting Gears

So if you are one of the eighty percent who doesn't enjoy what you are doing to make a living, and if I asked you why you are doing something you don't enjoy, what would your answer be? The most common answer I hear from people goes something like this, "Well, okay, I don't really like my job, but it pays the bills. Besides I'm not sure what it is I really want to do anyway." And there's the problem. They don't know what they want to do. Why? Simply because they have focused on the objects on the shores of life more than they have on the currents of Love within themselves and they have been pulled out of their boats. They have been focusing on what they don't want so much that there is no room or space for them to see what they do want. They are now so accustomed to doing what they know how to do that they are afraid to try something new. Their fear has them completely paralyzed. They are no longer living, but merely existing, doing whatever is necessary to get by. I don't choose to live that way.

In the career workshops I hold, I sometimes ask people to make two lists. One reads, "Things I Don't Want to Do in My Life". The other reads, "Things I Do Want to Do in My Life." Inevitably, the "don't want" list is much longer than the "do want" list. This demonstrates where their focus has been directed. <u>Knowing what you don't want and a quarter will buy you a glass of water</u>. It doesn't change a thing. Open a space within to see and feel what you do want. Then go for it!

Finding What You Want

There are processes I use to find out what it is that I want from life that I would like to share with you. I don't know if they will work for you, but they have worked for me. I was one of those people who said that I didn't know what I really wanted for many years. I had truly been pulled out of my boat. But after the experience at the stop light I knew it was time to start looking in other places for answers to my life. <u>I learned to look inside of myself</u>. Since then Love has shown me many answers. They had been there all along. I just chose to overlook them.

The first step I would suggest is a return to your childhood. Go back and search for the things that you truly enjoyed doing as a child. Perhaps it had something to do with nature, the sea, the forest, or animals. Maybe it was helping your mother prepare meals or helping your father repair the car or remodel a room in your home. We all experienced different activities in our childhood and the ones you enjoyed doing the most or the ones you always dreamed about doing when you "grew up" were Love's messages to you about what direction and steps you should take later in life. These are the areas upon which you should focus your attention. These are the things you probably love the most. These are the things that you, by nature, are about.

Another helpful process is to make a list of the people in your life you admire the most--the people you hold in the highest regard. What do they do for a living? Perhaps you admire a teacher you had in high school, your mother or father, an uncle who owned a farm, or anyone else. The people you most admire usually indicate what you most admire. Answers about what we truly want out of life come by searching our hearts and feelings. Is it possible that as a woman climbing the corporate ladder and finding no satisfaction, that what you really want is to be a good mother to your children and you have none, or vice versa? Or perhaps you've always wanted to be a forest ranger and you're a banker.

Over the years I buried my feelings so deeply it was difficult to uncover them. I had listened to so many voices outside of myself for so long that I began to believe that these voices were my voices and that they were speaking my feelings. But in time and with work, I began to get through the garbage and get in touch with me. And as I did I encountered a problem that I had to deal with. The problem was centered around my beliefs. You too might encounter the same problem and start making statements to yourself such as, "But I'm too old to start over." Or, "I don't have enough money to do what I want. Or, "I don't have the proper education." Or, "I have invested so much in my present career. How can I change now?" Well, no one says you have to, but as long as you are alive, it's never too late. And if you have invested so much into something that has brought you no joy or satisfaction in the past, is investing more into it going to bring you joy in the future?

The fears we can create when confronted with change are awesome. We can run to the future and make up all kinds of nightmares about things that could go wrong, and never focus on what could go right, or vice versa. And we can create so much fear that we do nothing. Is that what you want? More of the same? Or do you want to trust your feelings, go through the fear, and become all that you can possibly become? Love has brought you this far, and Love has not and will not ever give up on you. Trust it! Trust your feelings and act on them.

Perhaps a question will come up for you that goes something like this, "Well, okay, I know what I want to do, but how do I go about changing careers?" Whatever you did to get into the career you are in now obviously worked, so that's probably a good place to start. Retrace the steps you took to get where you are now, but this time with your attention focused on what you <u>love</u> rather than what you thought would be a good way to pay the bills. If that doesn't work, pray! Love will answer your prayers and show you options. If prayer is a concept that is hard for you to deal with, then meditate. Search your heart and feelings. Go to a place where you will not be disturbed and feel and listen. Answers will come. Doorways will open. Opportunities will arise.

And don't give up. In this "I want it yesterday," consumer oriented society patience is something that most of us lack. Love has great patience. Look at all the patience it has exercised with you. Be patient with yourself.

Or perhaps you enjoy what you are presently doing in your career, but you always wanted to play a musical instrument and never learned how. You can learn how! You simply have to find a good teacher, take lessons, and practice. Maturity and age do have virtues. You could probably learn to play much more easily now than you could have when you were a child. It just takes a little effort.

<u>Power is the ability to act</u>. Inaction is plain, simple laziness! In his book, <u>The Road Less Traveled</u>, Dr. M. Scott Peck gives a brilliant discussion on laziness and the law of entropy, the natural tendency for systems to deteriorate. In other words, water always runs downhill. It takes the course of least resistance. Peck states that,

> *Being about spiritual growth, this book is inevitably about the other side of the same coin: The impediments to spiritual growth. Ultimately there is only the one impediment, and that is laziness. If we overcome laziness, all the other impediments will be overcome. If we do not overcome laziness, none of the others will be hurdled. So this is also a book about laziness. In examining discipline we were considering the laziness of attempting to avoid necessary suffering, or taking the easy way out. In examining love we were also examining the fact that non-love is the unwillingness to extend one's self. Laziness is love's opposite. Spiritual growth is effortful, as we have been reminded again and again. We are now at a position from which we can examine the*

nature of laziness in perspective and realize that laziness is the force of entropy as it manifests itself in the lives of us all.

He goes on to state that the original sin was laziness.

> *The story suggests that God was in the habit of 'walking in the garden in the cool of the day' and that there were open channels of communication between Him and man. But if this was so, then why was it that Adam and Eve, separately or together, before or after the serpent's urging, did not say to God, 'We're curious as to why You don't want us to eat any of the fruit of the tree of the knowledge of good and evil. We really like it here, and we don't want to seem ungrateful, but Your law on this matter doesn't make much sense to us, and we'd really appreciate it if you explained it to us?' But of course they did not say this. Instead they went ahead and broke God's law without ever understanding the reason behind the law, without taking the effort to challenge God directly, question his authority or even communicate with Him on a reasonably adult level. They listened to the serpent, but they failed to get God's side of the story before they acted. Why this failure? Why was no step taken between the temptation and the action? It is this missing step that is the essence of sin. The step missing is the step of debate. Adam and Eve could have set up a debate between the serpent and God, but in failing to do so they failed to obtain God's side of the question. The debate between the serpent and God is symbolic of the dialogue between good and evil which can and should occur within the minds of human beings. Our failure to conduct--or to conduct fully and wholeheartedly--this internal debate between good and evil is the cause of those evil actions that constitute sin. In debating the wisdom of a proposed course of action, human beings routinely fail to obtain God's side of the issue. They fail to consult or listen to the God within them, the knowledge of rightness which inherently resides within the minds of all mankind. We make this failure because we are lazy. It is work to hold these internal debates. They require time and energy just to conduct them. And if we take them seriously--if we seriously listen to this 'God within us'--we usually find ourselves being urged to take the more difficult path, the path of more effort rather than less. To conduct the debate is to open ourselves to suffering and struggle. Each and every one of us, more or less frequently, will hold back from this work, will also seek to avoid this painful step. Like Adam and Eve, and every one of our ancestors before us, we are all lazy.*

If you want to make changes in your life, you can. Start by searching for what it is you really want in life. Let the search begin within your heart. When answers come, act upon them. Ask Love--the God within you--for help and guidance and you will receive it.

MONEY

Abundance is everywhere.

Scarcity is an illusion.

In giving, I receive a hundred fold.

I have all I need to be happy now.

We've all heard the old adage, "Money is the root of all evil". I would like to rephrase it and say that addiction to money and what it can buy can be the cause of much unhappiness. Man originally devised money to facilitate commercial trade. It can also be seen as a measure of one's creativity and effort. We work to make money to purchase the necessities of life; i.e., food, shelter, clothing to protect us from the elements, recreation, etc. But the society in which we live has become so consumer oriented that many of us have become very confused about what money is and have developed a belief or assumption that money is, or can buy, happiness. I, too, believed this, but Love in its infinite wisdom and patience has since given me the necessary experience to see otherwise.

Being Honest with Yourself

Look around you. If you live in a city, your only source of food is the supermarket. You work in a city because you can make more money to buy more "stuff," as George Carlin would say, and think that some day when you have enough "stuff," you'll finally be happy. You think your source of happiness will come from outside of you. You think your means is different from your end. Love has taught me that happiness can only come from the source and creator of my emotions and feelings, me. Until your means become your end, you will never realize the results of your intention, because you are simply not clear about your intention, no matter how vehemently you say you are. There is absolutely nothing outside of you that can bring you joy and happiness, including money and everything it can buy. Love is the only thing can bring real joy into your life. As you love yourself and others more fully, the natural consequence is a feeling of happiness.

Don't misunderstand what I am saying. In today's society money is a necessity. We need to purchase the necessities of life because we have set up a system of trade that does not function without it. But it is certainly not a perfect system. Have you ever thought what would happen in the large cities we have built, like Los Angeles, New York, Tokyo, Paris, London, or Mexico City, if there were a drought in the United States that lasted for two or three years, as has happened in parts of Africa? We have set up a means of survival that would collapse if Nature deviated from what we call normal for a few short years. And we have done all of this because of our addiction to money.

The Price of Global Unconciousness

We live on a planet whose population is increasing by one hundred million human beings every 365 days. By the year 2000 there will be 6.2 billion of us living some kind of life here on earth. The need for a complete renewal of this planet's energy production system is as undeniable as it is incomprehensible. The equatorial rain forests regulating the planet's climate have been and continue to be destroyed on a daily basis. The ozone layers surrounding the earth are being destroyed at a frightening rate. There are 50,000 to 75,000 nuclear warheads located at various places on the face of the earth, each one of which has sixty-six times the explosive force of the bomb that destroyed Hiroshima.

We may be the planet's dominant species, but we know less about how to coexist with ourselves and other life forms now than ever before. We have the most sophisticated technologies of all time, yet we are at the greatest peril of doing away with ourselves. And we have created this situation because we have blinded ourselves by our addiction to money, greed and a fantasy about the imagined power of money and what it can buy.

For many years I was in the top two to three percent of income in the world, and I was sure that money could buy happiness. Then Love allowed me to experience the tremendous pain and agony of bankruptcy, and I began to look at money in a different light.

Mohandas K. Gandhi, after having reached great financial success in his younger years, had some things to say about money that I think would be helpful to cite at this point.

"How heavy is the toll of sins and wrongs that wealth, power and prestige exact from man. "

"Happiness, the goal to which we all are striving, is reached by endeavoring to make the lives of others happy, and if by removing the luxuries of life we can lighten the burdens of others...surely the simplification of our wants is a thing greatly to be desired. And so, if instead of supposing that we must become hermits and dwellers in caves in order to practice simplicity, we set about simplifying our affairs, each according to his own convictions and opportunity, much good will result and the simple life will at once be established."

"Formerly, men were made slaves under physical compulsion; now they are enslaved by the temptation of money and of the luxuries that money can buy."

And finally, "I must say that there is a subtle self-conceit in the insistence that we should work without drawing any allowance. There is no humiliation in receiving an allowance for one's livelihood, but a clear duty. "

I think all of us could learn something from these teachings if we would be honest with ourselves. I especially think that our politicians would do well to adhere to these basic truths about money.

Possessions

If you search your heart, Love will show you what, "each according to his own convictions and opportunity..." means for you. This is a very important concept. I do not believe that a rich man should be judged a bad man, but I do believe that it is easier in most cases, "for a camel to pass through the eye of a needle than a rich man to enter the Kingdom of Heaven," the Kingdom of Love, Truth, and Happiness. There is nothing wrong with having a lot of money. To the contrary, much good can be done with large sums of money. But the chances of becoming confused, attached, and identifying with a great number of material possessions is awesome. When we become overly concerned with and attached to, our possessions or money we will be living in the fear of losing them and our happiness will diminish. The more possessions we own the more we are owned by them. There is great power in simplicity. Live simply and at peace with yourself.

May I suggest that the next time you just have to buy something that you stop and consider why you want it so badly? Remember all of the other material possessions you just couldn't live without? When was the last time they brought you any joy? Can you wait until you know what it is you really want before you rush out to spend your resources? Try it! Take a good look at yourself in relationship to your money.

Credit

Take a moment and look at your relationship to credit and your ability to borrow money. What does it mean to you to have good credit? I found that much of my imagined identity was about my good credit or my borrowing power. It had become an extension of my ego. And when that happens we're headed for a collision with reality. We're flirting with financial disaster.

Credit has put many of us into deep financial holes. Operating on borrowed money has placed many communities, countries, states and our own federal government into bankruptcy; yet we refuse to admit it.

If our relationship to money is a healthy one, much good can come from monies properly channeled. Money can be seen as a unit of creativity. The more money you have, the more creative you have been.

With money people can be fed and clothed. Research can be done at our universities and other institutes of learning. Our children can be educated. Orphans and senior citizens can be cared for. But when money is spent unconsciously, thinking that it will bring happiness through pleasure and the immediate gratification of unbridled and imagined needs, great waste is created and much harm done in our individual lives and on a collective basis.

One basic principle I have learned to live by is, "If I don't have the cash to buy it, I don't need it." And most of the time, even if I have the cash, I still don't need it.

Abundance or Scarcity

I believe that Love could create a state of wealth and prosperity on this planet the likes of which we can only imagine in our dreams, if we could each learn to exercise a little self-discipline when it comes to spending our resources. My experience has been that there is never a lack of money in our lives. There is however a great deal of laziness, very little self control and a tremendous need for more independent thinking and creative ideas.

If you show me an idea, product, or service of great significance that could benefit mankind as a whole, I will show you money in all shapes and sizes being attracted to it. There is plenty of money just waiting to be invested in a solid, creative and innovative idea. I am sure that if you looked honestly, you would find this to be true.

If you want to start your own business, or do something of a charitable nature in your community to be of service to your brothers and sisters, and it is what the Love within you is directing you to do, I promise you will find a way to secure sufficient monies, if you look hard enough. If you don't find it, reevaluate the idea, your feelings, and your motivation. Money runs to great ideas. It runs away from poor ones. It is simply the law of attraction. Like attracts like.

So perhaps it's time you take a good look at what you want to do with the rest of your life and how the money you have attracted into your life, the money that Love has created for you, could best be spent. If you are living from a belief of scarcity, scarcity is what you will experience. If you are living in Love and Truth, abundance will be all around you.

OUR BODIES OF SPIRIT
AND MATTER

I am in control of myself.

I love my body.

I am beautiful in all ways.

I enjoy being healthy.

I enjoy taking care of myself physically.

Once as I was searching for a deeper understanding of myself, Love shared a mental scene with me concerning our physical bodies. I saw in my mind's eye a beautiful sphere of warm, radiant Light. This Light was symbolic of the Love of God. There was a triangular lens, or prism, in front of the Light, and as the Light shown through the prism, it fragmented into all of the beautiful colors of the rainbow. Within these many colors were thousands of tiny particles of Light. It was beautiful. And Love spoke to me, saying that each particle of Light was a living Soul, or Spirit. Each of these Light particles created a field of Loving energy and influence unto itself. Separate, yet part of the whole. A connected wave of Light, and at the same time an individual particle. This is what our scientists and physicists have found light to be. Depending on the frame of reference or the manner in which light is observed, it is either a wave or a particle. And therefore both at the same time.

These small particles of Light created electro-magnetic fields which attracted elemental matter unto them, much like a magnet attracts and aligns iron shavings into beautiful shapes and forms around itself. The forms created by the fields of energy surrounding these individuated particles of Light are our bodies.

Our bodies are wonderful instruments for perceiving and gathering information. Our senses of touch, taste, sight, smell, and hearing are awe inspiring. These senses allow us to enjoy many marvelous experiences and sensations. <u>And their attraction to matter is tremendously powerful</u>.

Questioning our Motives

I have found it has been crucial in my life to constantly question the source of my desires or motivation. By this I mean is my Higher Self directing me, or am I being driven by some sort of addiction to sensual or material pleasure? The difference is ever so subtle, but very important. We must be constantly vigilant of our senses and consciously aware of our motivation when making decisions or choices in our lives. When I have made decisions based on my addictions or my attraction to material or sensual gratification rather than my intuition, the results have been less than satisfactory and at times disastrous.

For example, have you ever looked at shopping for clothing as a sensual experience? Clothing gives us protection from the environment, but we also buy clothing that is pleasing to our senses of touch and sight. I'm sure you all know shopping junkies. Searching for happiness outside of ourselves in such ways creates many problems. Eating our favorite foods can be a very satisfying experience, as well as a means of maintaining our bodies. But when eating becomes an obsession, watch out. Living with and understanding our five senses and physical bodies is a question of balance. And it is very important that we maintain balance in our lives. When working properly, our bodies can carry out amazing tasks for years. But when abused or neglected, they, like any machine, eventually break down.

Learning About our Bodies

Part of becoming more conscious is becoming more aware of your physical body and the feelings and thoughts you experience with your body. One day I realized that I knew more about the different parts of a car and how they work than I knew about myself. For example, do you know where your adrenal glands are located in your body and what their purpose is in relationship to the whole? Or what about your pituitary gland, your pineal gland, your pancreas or liver? Could you explain to another person why your white blood cell count increases during an illness and what their function is? If you can, great. If not, acknowledge your lack of understanding and learn more about your body. If your car's oil needs changing, you probably know how to change it. But if your kidney stops functioning, would you have any idea what to do or what could be wrong? Most of us take more and better care of our material possessions than we do our bodies. Why? Disregard for our physical bodies is simply a symptom of not loving ourselves wholly and completely. If we hold a belief that we are unlovable or inferior in any way, chances are that we will not want to know about or care for ourselves physically.

As I learned to love myself more deeply, changes began to occur outwardly. I lost the desire to use drugs and alcohol. I began exercising and lost 40 pounds. I even began to enjoy exercising. As this was occurring I began to be more aware of the messages my body was sending me and began to change my diet. And my body loved it. I found myself having more energy and needing less sleep. I also noticed that I was much less vulnerable to mood changes. My depression and feelings of loneliness began to disappear, and I started to feel "good" almost all of the time. It was wonderful to be healthy. My thoughts and emotions became clearer. I began to be more sensitive to the subtle whisperings that Love was sharing with me. Taking care of myself physically became a joy, rather than a job. And the benefits were marvelous. It was like having a whole new outlook on life. Taking better care of yourself physically is something I would recommend to anyone and gaining a better understanding of your body is essential if you are to care for it properly.

Your physical body consists of the material elements your Spirit has called up to dance in its vibrational field of Love. Expressing Love for your body is a must if you are to achieve alignment or unity with the Universe. When your spirit and body are in alignment and working together in a healthy, harmonious manner, all things are possible. John Wheeler, one of the world's leading physicists, proposes that perhaps all there is in the universe is <u>information flowing through fields</u>, and the way it works is just <u>magic</u>. I would suggest that the information is Truth and the field through which it flows is Love. Combined, the two are what man calls God. When we are in alignment with Love, or God, all information necessary to live a fulfilling life can be channeled through and received by our bodies. When we are in alignment, all that is necessary is to sit back and enjoy the <u>magic</u>.

I sometimes think of our bodies as radio transmitting and receiving stations. When everything is working properly the signals can be received, processed, and transmitted clearly and easily. But when we are in a state of disease we block the signals or messages being sent to us by the Universe.

In western society we do a great many things to block the signals and clog the airwaves. So let me suggest a few guidelines for your physical health. And note how you respond emotionally as you read these guidelines. If they are upsetting to you in any way, perhaps you are uncovering more addictions. But first consider a paradox.

Another Paradox

Maintaining good physical health is vital to becoming all that we can become. Yet I firmly believe that one should never give something up through stern or austere living. In other words, I don't think that you should beat yourself into submission. Anything you have to drive yourself to give up will only come back to haunt you later, because the desire, the root of the problem, has not been dealt with. You are only chopping away at the branches by using such means. As long as one obtains inner comfort from anything, whether it be drugs, alcohol, cigarettes, sex, or anything else, one should continue to enjoy it. It is better to enjoy with the body than to be wallowing in the thought of such enjoyment in the mind. You should only give a thing up when you have found some other condition you desire more and this thing is stopping you from attaining your new desire. If you have problems with substances such as drugs, alcohol, etc., be conscious of your experience when you are using them. Notice how they make you feel. But sometimes by pruning the branches a little we can more clearly see the root. So let's do some pruning.

Using Common Sense

Stop eating refined sugar. Sugar is the second or third most widely-used ingredient in most processed foods. It's in almost everything and it does nothing but add calories to your diet and puts your body in a constant state of stress management. It slowly kills you. Stop drinking carbonated, sweetened beverages, and anything else that has refined sugar as an additive. You probably think that you just couldn't live without sugar, but after about two weeks without it, if you taste something that has been heavily sweetened, it will gag you. Start reading the labels on the food you buy. There are many food manufacturers who no longer use sugar. It just takes a little effort on your part. Express some love for yourself.

Second, quit eating salt. There is plenty of salt in wholesome, natural foods already. You don't need any more. And after about two weeks you will lose your acquired taste for salt, just as you did for sugar.

Third, stop drinking alcoholic beverages. If you drink and would argue that you don't have a drinking problem, chances are that you do. Every ounce of alcohol you consume kills brain cells, damages your liver, heart and kidneys, and negatively affects every other cell in your body. If you think you need to drink to have fun, you have a drinking problem.

Fourth, if you smoke or use drugs, quit. If you need help, get it. But get clear about your intention and quit. And remember, don't beat yourself up over any of this. Creating guilt and inflicting it upon yourself doesn't work. Love yourself just as you are, and start talking to yourself in more loving ways. Say things like, "I love myself too much to smoke, drink or do drugs," or whatever it is you do that is harmful. As you express this verbal love to yourself on a daily basis, in time your outer reality will come into alignment with your new inner reality.

Fifth, stop using products that contain caffeine. That means coffee, caffinated, carbonated beverages, and many of the drugs you purchase. Caffeine, like sugar, puts your blood sugar on a roller coaster ride. Your body is constantly trying to manage stress because of the foods you eat which contain sugar or caffeine. You are simply wearing your body and organs out by using them.

Sixth, stop eating fried foods. Foods fried in animal fat contain enormous amounts of cholesterol. They simply are not good for you. Broil or bake your foods.

Seventh, cut down on red meats. Eat more fish and poultry. Another good source of protein is soy or tofu. There are many good recipe books one can purchase which teach how to use these foodstuffs. Be open to possibilities.

Eighth, decrease your fat intake by using less dairy products and when you do use them, use products such as low-fat milk or cheeses.

Start eating three regular meals a day. These meals should consist of wholesome, natural foods. Eat oatmeal or Cream of Wheat for breakfast, with fruit rather than sugar.

Introduce more fresh fruits and vegetables into your diet. These should be the mainstay of your diet. Drink water; you'll be amazed at how good it tastes with a slice of lemon or lime. If a food is natural and fresh, it's probably good for you. If it's processed, it probably isn't.

And exercise fifteen or twenty minutes a day. There are twenty-four hours in each day. Is taking twenty minutes to exercise daily too much to ask of anyone? So many of us are like little children pouting because we can't have what we want. This is your life we are talking about. Live it to the fullest. Go for a walk with your spouse or children for twenty minutes. You will probably enjoy the time together, along with the exercise. The benefits will amaze you. You will even begin to like it after awhile. Your mood changes will become less severe. You will find that you experience much less depression and anxiety in your life. And you will just feel better all of the time.

All you have to do is begin. Go shopping and buy some healthy food. Then eat it. Buy a book called <u>Medical Makeover</u> by Dr. Robert M. Giller. It is possibly the best book written on overall, general good health. Another I would recommend is <u>Awaken Healing Energy Through the TAO</u> by Mantak Chia. This book takes a comprehensive look at our spiritual bodies, and how our energy fields function and flow. You can learn to increase the flow of Love, the life force itself, with some simple exercises.

Begin by beginning! Love yourself. Don't beat yourself up for where you are now. If you smoke, smoke and love yourself, cigarettes and all. When you're ready to quit, you will. If you have a drug or alcohol problem, acknowledge it and love yourself. The problems will go away as you learn to follow your intuition and express more love towards yourself. Listen to your intuition. Perhaps it will tell you to seek help at some sort of rehabilitation center or share other ways with you that will assist you in your growth. Listen and act on what it tells you. If you're overweight, great! Love yourself. Forgive yourself and know that you don't have to be overweight if you choose not to be. The choice is yours, just as it has always been.

Learn to listen to your body. If it is craving a certain type of food, and you are no longer addicted to sugars, salt, drugs or other unhealthy substances, it is telling you that it needs that type of food. As you learn to listen to what your body is telling you, you will become very efficient at it. Sometimes your body will tell you that it needs a nap. Take one. A cup of coffee might pep you up for awhile, but you will be even more worn out later. Other times your body might tell you to take the day off and go for a walk in the mountains or spend the day at home reading a book by the fireplace. Listen to it and wonderful things will begin to happen.

Love can change lives. I know because Love has changed mine. Love is all you need, because in reality, Love is all there is. You simply have to become conscious of its presence in your life and stop making up all kinds of stories, illusions, in an attempt to deny its existence. Love of self can bring about miracles in your life. And achieving a better state of physical health, to me, is miraculous. I truly believe that if we could learn to listen to our bodies more effectively, death and disease, as we know them now would cease. We could live three lifetimes in the same body, or more, if we chose to. So love yourself. Become aware of what you eat, and how you feel and think about your body. Love your body just as it is. Do what you know would be in your own best interest, and start enjoying your life to the fullest.

SEXUALITY

I was born in the image and likeness

of God, Goddess, All That Is.

I was born a sexual being and

I love myself for being this way.

I own and embrace my sexuality.

I accept my sexuality.

I love my sexuality.

To be sexual, is to be God.

In central India there lives a tribe of healthy, happy people known as the Abujmarhia. The Abujmarhia enjoy a pollution-free environment, a wholesome natural diet, relaxed, but occasionally strenuous work in the fields during the day, dancing and storytelling by evening, and plenty of rest. They also enjoy abundantly loving sexual relationships beginning premaritally in early adolescence. As children they are allowed to play together sexually if they desire to do so. Nothing sexual is repressed. They do not teach their children to abstain from sex, but rather to embrace their sexuality and enjoy it. They are taught to love one another and themselves as the sexual beings they are by nature.

In this tribe there is no venereal disease. There is no child molestation or child abuse. There is no spousal abuse or incest. The members of the tribe are not seen as possessions which another owns. This tribe does not make or engage in war. And cancer is unknown to them. Their lives are joyous, full, happy and abundant. They have absolutely no fear or inner conflict where their sexuality is concerned. What an example they are.

The Inner War

In western society it is altogether a different story. From childhood most of us are taught to fear and repress our sexuality. We are taught that it is sinful, immoral, nasty, bad, dirty, and just basically an awful thing to think about, let alone do. We are taught to repress any sexual thoughts and not to engage in sexual activity until we are legally married. After we enter into this contractual agreement it is then all right to engage in sexual activity. The problem lies in overcoming twenty or thirty years of negative programming where sex is concerned if our marriages are ever going to work. Our marriages are contractual agreements of ownership. We actually believe that we own one another physically and sexually. Maritial infidelity is considered sinful and grounds for divorce, yet it is commomplace. And in our divorces we divide up the property, demonstrating the ownership intended in the original marital contract.

In western society child abuse, child molestation, spousal abuse, abortion, rape, venereal disease, marital infidelity and incest are everywhere. We don't like to admit this, but it's the truth.

In western society many of our lives are filled with stress and inner conflict. Heart attacks, ulcers, high blood pressure and cancer are common. And we are out to westernize the entire world because we believe everyone else should live this wonderful lifestyle we have created for ourselves.

Friends, it's time to wake up and acknowledge that we as a society are sick. We are filled with inner conflict and turmoil and much of it is caused by not understanding our own sexuality and not loving ourselves for the sexual beings we are. This inner conflict is manifested outwardly in many ways. Perhaps the most significant is war. We spend more money and resources on preparing for war than any other nation in the world. We also supply most of the arms used to fight the wars going on around the world. And we are too blind to see the roots of our unconsciously created nightmares.

Sex is a natural, God-given characteristic. It is fun, enjoyable, healthy and very powerful. It is not sinful, immoral, bad, or nasty. To state or believe otherwise is simply another way of not loving yourself to the fullest. It is neurotic, sick and damaging to not love yourself just as you are. And you were born a sexual being. Love yourself for being born that way.

Experience and Consequence

I can remember being curious about my sexuality at the age of four or five. One morning I was playing with the little girl next door. She got undressed, I got undressed and we were ready to do something. It's just that neither of us knew what it was we were ready to do. And we didn't care at all that we were naked on my front porch in view of the whole world. It was fun, exciting, playful and natural. We were both having a great time. About six months later my mother caught us doing the same thing in my basement and proceeded to literally beat the hell out of us. She told us that we were nasty, bad, awful, little people, and should never do what we were doing again. From that point on my life was never the same.

The spanking certainly didn't curtail my sexual activity, but it did make me go into hiding when I expressed it. I continued to engage in my sexual behavior, but I did so in the constant fear of being found out and with a huge amount of guilt associated with it. I was becoming neurotic where my own sexuality was concerned, just as my mother had become neurotic about hers.

A year later as I turned a corner in my home I saw my mother kissing a man who wasn't my father. Inside I remember the anger and confusion welling up inside of me concerning both sex and women. How could my mother condemn me for my sexual feelings yet express her own in such contradictory ways? My own inner war was beginning to rage and the neurosis was becoming ever greater.

As I grew older I realized that I was not the only little boy in this situation. My friends were in identical ones. Their parents were teaching them to repress their sexuality and feel guilty about it. Yet they were driven by nature to express it. And they did so in many different ways. I once watched my cousin attempt to have sex with a young horse and I remember how strange this seemed to me, yet I knew that nothing was wrong with my cousin. He was just sexually curious and had no other means of expression.

I remember being twelve years old and going to Idaho for the weekend with a very kind man who had befriended me. We spent the evening at the home of a family he knew. During the night I was suddenly awakened to find his hand massaging my leg. I jumped out of bed and ran to the bathroom. I was very nervous and tried to figure out what was going on. I thought he must be dreaming that he was in bed with his wife, but a small voice within me told me otherwise. I spent the rest of the night on top of the covers. This experience upset me badly and to this day I feel uncomfortable when I think of sleeping in the same bed with another man. And over the years I have learned to feel sorry for my friend. He was a homosexual, but had hidden it his entire life. The inner turmoil and pain he experienced throughout his life must have been tremendous.

Later in my teens I began to drink and do drugs excessively. I now realize that one of the reasons I turned to these things was that I was searching for a way to escape from the confusion I was experiencing concerning my own sexuality. But there was no escape. My sexual experiences during these years were very unconscious ones. I was always under the influence of drugs or alcohol and I was becoming addicted to sex as a means to avoid my inner pain. I no longer, experienced it as a natural, conscious expression of my human beingness.

During this time there were no adults in my life who understood their own sexuality to counsel or assist me in understanding mine. And all of my sexual activity took place in hiding. I was hiding from my parents, my society and some god that I had been told would punish such behavior. All the while I felt as if I was doing something wrong and that something was wrong with me. I now know that nothing was wrong with me.

Repression Doesn't Work

Any emotion that is repressed will eventually seek manifestation at a later date. What you resist emotionally, persists. Any emotion that is acknowledged and experienced in the moment one feels that emotion will dissipate and be gone. And by experiencing the emotion I don't mean you need to act out the emotion. Simply feel the emotion fully. Own it, experience it, and it will dissolve. By teaching your children to repress their own natural sexuality you are creating a time bomb that is some day going to explode. When it does the results will not be pleasant for them or the people in their lives.

In my mid-twenties I broke my wife's heart because of marital infidelity. And she was doing same thing. The other people we were having sex with were dealing with the same neurotic problems. We were all having sex with people besides our spouses and lying about the truth of our experience, and hating ourselves for doing it. And we were creating all of this pain in our lives simply because we wouldn't acknowledge that we were sexual beings looking for answers to our own sexuality, and love ourselves for doing so.

Love or Neurosis

Look at the state of your life right now. Isn't it true that you are scared to death at the thought of your spouse or lover having sex with someone else? And fear is not love. Fear in a relationship is a manifestation of neurotic, co-dependency, and addictive possessiveness or ownership. We're sick and afraid to acknowledge our sickness. I am not saying that we should be out having wild sexual orgies with one another. If we would simply teach our children as children that sexuality is a natural part of being human, most, if not all of the sexual problems we experience as adults would never arise.

A Wakeup Call

The topic of venereal disease is something that also needs to be discussed. Syphilis is thought to have come from sheep. AIDS has been linked to monkeys in Haiti and parts of Africa. Because we have taught our children to repress their sexuality and hate themselves for being sexual a few of our species have turned to animals to express and discover their sexuality. And I believe this is far more common than any of us realize. By engaging in such behavior these individuals have infected our species not only with diseases like syphilis but now the AIDS virus that could wipe out millions upon millions of human beings.

When are we going to wake up? The answer is not in repressing our sexuality but in owning it and embracing it for what it is. Sex is not sinful. It is natural, enjoyable, and very powerful. It can create life. It can now also destroy life. Isn't it time that we begin to understand our sexuality and solve the sexual problems that plague our society? The way we have been going about it simply doesn't work.

A Paradigm Shift

Let me explain more fully who we are and how we work as human beings in a way that might not be familiar, yet is perhaps the most precise explanation possible. I believe this understanding could help us in our sexual discovery.

As human beings we are similar to musical instruments. Our spirits and bodies are vibrating particles of spiritual energy and matter. These pulsating vibrations create sound or music. And we each vibrate at different levels or frequencies. We therefore create different musical notes and harmonies. We each have different tonal qualities. The more consciously aware we become the more finely tuned we become as individual instruments and the clarity of our vibrations, our musical intonations, becomes much brighter.

A musical chord is created by combining three notes of a musical scale. There are five master traids or types of chords. There are major, minor, augmented, diminished and suspended chords. This gives us a wide range of musical possibilities. But for the purpose of demonstration let's use a major chord. The 1, 3 and 5 notes of any scale create a major chord. For example, if we use an A scale, the notes in the scale are ABC#DEF#G#A. The first, third and fifth notes of the scale give us an A chord. A, C# and E creates the chord. So any time these three notes are played together an A chord is created. But by playing them in different sequences we can create the same chord with a slightly different flavor or color. This is referred to as the <u>voicing</u> of the chord. For example, if we were to play AAC#EC#, the voicing would be 1, 1, 3, 5, 3. This is still an A chord, but with a variation on the voicing of the chord, which gives the chord the variation in musical color.

As humans, being musical, we resonate different musical chords as well as different voicings. These vibrations can be heard or sensed as music or sound if we are conscious and sensitive enough to do so. These vibrations can also be seen in our auras. The electro-magnetic fields which surround us, our auras, vibrate at the same frequencies and can be seen if we are conscious in this area of perception. These physical vibrations, or waves, create different colors. Color is simply light waves of varying frequencies. So there are two ways in which you can recognize similar souls as you become more conscious and develop your inherent abilities. First you can hear the vibration or music of their soul, and secondly you can see the similarity in the aura of the person. We already do this and on a much lower level of consciousness in the act of "falling in love."

A sexual experience with someone who vibrates very differently from yourself might feel good physically, but emotionally, mentally, spiritually or vibrationally the two of you would be out of harmony. In such encounters there is simply not a fullness created in the experience, nor can there be. But when sex is enjoyed by two people whose soul notes are very similar and in some cases identical, a whole new experience is created. A merging of mind, body and spirit is experienced which words cannot describe. It is a telepathic, clairvoyant experience of immense proportions. After one has had such an experience there is simply no longer any desire for sexual encounters which would be less satisfying. But if one has never had lesser experiences on a conscious level with others who create dissimilar musical chords and voicings, they have nothing to compare it with. They simply wouldn't understand the difference between harmonic sex and disharmonic sex. Their own sexuality might never be completely understood and their lives might be filled with confusion and curiosity. They might constantly be wondering what sex with someone else would be like. And my observations have been that when this occurs, the curiosity will eventually be satisfied. When done in later life the effects of satisfying their curiousity can be devastating.

For people who just don't have a great amount of sexual energy or curiosity this might never be an obstacle. But if those who do could come to understand their sexuality at an age when pregnancy was not yet possible or in adolescence under the guidance and supervision of parents and counselors, marital infidelity would not be a problem. But because we hold sex as sinful and something that should be repressed, when we finally do go in search of our sexuality as adults, we create all kinds of unnecessary pain in our lives and in the lives of others. We then condemn one another for trying to discover our own sexuality which causes us once again to hide our sexual behavior. Many people turn to children to discover and express their sexual drives. This is so unfortunate. If we could simply learn to be open and honest about our sexual feelings with ourselves and others such sexual pitfalls could be avoided.

Children

If you are a parent and have children who are expressing a lot of sexual energy, don't tell them it is bad and that they shouldn't do it. Be open with them concerning their sexuality. Talk with them openly and honestly. Counsel them concerning the natural consequences of their sexual activity. You are not going to stop them if they decide to have sex. You are only going to cause them to hide their behavior and break down the lines of communication between you if you impose some sort of strict morality on them. But you could certainly assist them in avoiding a tremendous amount of pain and confusion in their lives by being open and honest concerning their own sexuality. And not all children manifest this type of sexual energy. We all have different issues to deal with in our individual evolution and different lifetimes. But if you cause children who do have a lot of sexual energy or issues to hide their behavior and feel guilty about it, neurosis will set in. When this happens addictive patterns of behavior occur and the child will begin to see sex as something that is difficult to find, have or enjoy. They will begin to live from a belief of sexual scarcity rather than sexual abundance and be driven to get as much as they can whenever they can, and all the while hiding their behavior. They will begin to hold sex as a scarce commodity which they must secure and hold onto in any way possible. When this happens a conflict between the desire for sex and the belief that it is wrong will begin to rage within them. They may then turn to alcohol and drugs as a way to rid themselves of their inner confusion.

If you are not a parent and are thinking about becoming one, be sure that you are comfortable and secure in your own sexuality before you do. If you cannot talk openly and candidly about your own sexual activities, behavior, and feelings in any situation, be very clear about the fact that you do not understand your own sexuality. And it might be best to not have children until you do.

If you are an adult with a lot of sexual energy, explore your sexuality but do so with both eyes open. And I am not saying that you need to go out and have endless sexual encounters. AIDS can kill you. <u>Much, if not all, of your exploration can be done within yourself through meditation and contemplation.</u> If you then choose to have sexual encounters, make your sexual experiences conscious ones. You are powerful enough to consciously attract to you the experiences that would most benefit you. If you are trying to understand your sexuality, how much progress do you think you are going to make if your sexual experiences are done under the influence of drugs and alcohol with someone you pick up at a bar who is in the same condition? The sex might feel good physically, but what can you learn about yourself in such a state of mind? Be conscious. Be aware. Don't be an addict.

Being Honest about Your Sexuality

If you are homosexual or lesbian, love yourself for being the way you are and be open about it. I am not saying you have to be flagrant with your behavior, but be truthful. Self-honesty is perhaps the most essential step people can take in life if they are ever going to make their lives work. Be honest and truthful with yourself and others in every way possible. There is absolutely nothing wrong or sinful about being born with a natural sexual preference for someone of the same sex. And anyone that tells you differently is someone you don't need in your life. Such people do not understand themselves and are afraid of their own sexuality. Such people lack self love, are misguided in their own lives, and are simply projecting their own self hate and morality onto you in an attempt to be right about their beliefs. Anything you fear is something you do not understand. But if you are gay, please be conscious in your sexual discovery. You are in one of the highest risk groups possible to contract AIDS. And thinking that you have taken ample precautions is not enough. AIDS is transmitted through bodily fluids. Saliva is a bodily fluid. Saliva is transmitted through kissing. During intercourse small blood vessels can be broken and therefore the likelihood of transmission is much greater with intercourse than with kissing. And for the same reason the risk is much higher through anal intercourse than through vaginal intercourse. Is it worth taking such a chance with a casual sexual encounter? Is sexual gratification more meaningful than life itself? Ask someone who is dying from AIDS what their thoughts on the subject are. Ask a mother or father whose child is now dead because of this disease if they think sexual gratification is worth it. What more will it take until we understand who we are and what we have come to this planet to learn? How much pain and suffering will it take to teach us and bring us to consciousness?

Love is bringing us to an awareness of our awesome power as co-creators of Life and the great responsibilities which accompany this power. Be aware of what you do now, for as a powerful electron microscope need only move a few inches at its fulcrum to travel light years across the star systems, your actions now can create or destroy generations and worlds to come. Be sensitive to what Love is trying to teach us as a planet. Loosen the intensity of your focus on the daily problems you take so seriously and step back to observe the bigger picture, the greater Truth. Hold a small child in your arms and feel the presence of Love in your life and know the sacredness of Love and Life itself. Understand and embrace your creative power as a sexual being. Why would you ever want to put those you love at risk? Today when one has casual sexual relationships they are no longer having sex with just one person, but every person their partner has been with in the past. Don't allow an addiction to blot out your life, or the lives of your children and your children's children. Love is Life, and the outcome of your life is in your hands. Take a conscious look at the place sex holds in your life.

Your Focused Reality
    Once while I was sitting in my living room talking with a friend about the arguments I had had over the years with women concerning sexuality,

Love placed a picture in my mind. It was a simple pie graph and it symbolized the whole of a Loving relationship. A small section of this graph was cut out. I closed my eyes and asked my Higher Self what this meant, and it came to me that the missing part represented sex in a relationship. What I had been doing in my relationships was focusing so intently on the two percent that I hadn't even noticed the other ninety-eight percent. Look around you for a moment and notice all that is within your field of vision. Now take your hand and place it over your eyes, keeping your eyes open. What do you see besides your hand? This is what I had been doing with sex for years. I had focused so intently on the sex that I had blocked out the other considerations in healthy relationships. And it was perfect for my growth, but painful. Until I understood my own sexuality I was never able to have a healthy relationship. And repressing your sexuality will never allow you the opportunity to discover it.

By nature we are all wonderful, magnificent human beings. We are not born to be drunks, drug addicts, or sexual deviants. Jesus taught that we should become as little children. A child is born perfect. It takes years of neurotic programming by unconscious, self-despising, self-righteous, fearful adults to mess them up. And it is not a crime to be unconscious. When are we going to stop this insanity? Love yourself just as you are. Love your sexuality and explore your sexuality consciously with an open mind to understand it more fully.

And don't confuse sex with love or intimacy. I have found that premature sexual relationships actually block my ability to become intimate with another person. Such relationships are very easy to get into, but getting out can be very painful and very damaging to both people. The answers to your questions concerning sexuality lie within you as do all other answers to your life. Search within your heart for the answers. Discover all of who you are and when you do you will find that sex is just another aspect of you. It is a very beautiful, powerful part of your personality. It is not something that you should fear or run from. It is not love. It is sex. Yet it can be a very wonderful expression of your love for another person. And sex is not a panacea for loneliness or insecurity. As you experience your sexuality more completely I know that you will find as I have that your need to share it with the whole world will greatly diminish. And you will in time find someone to share it with in a way that will cause you to have no desire to share it with anyone else simply because together you create a symphony of Love which only the two of you possibly could.

FUTURING AND PASTING

I center my thoughts.

I am always where I am.

This is where I am supposed to be now.

I am happy.

I see good in all.

As children, much of our learning was motivated by fear. We heard the voices of our parents and others say things that went something like this:

"Just wait until your father gets home."
"If you're not back by midnight, you'll never drive the car again."
"If you don't eat all of the food on your plate, you'll never watch
TV again, and you'll spend the rest of your life in your bedroom."

And so on and so on.

Our young minds rushed to the future, and we imagined all types of horrors that could befall us. We also heard other voices that drew us into the past, such as:

"How could you have done such a thing?"
"Don't you know that good girls/boys don't do that?"
"You should feel awful for having said that to your mother."
"I can't believe you did that."

And so on and so on.

Now our parents and teachers meant well when they attempted to motivate change in our lives by saying these things. They had been taught in the same ways and were simply doing what they knew how to do. And sometimes it worked. But what was also taking place was that a devastating addictive pattern was being set up; an addiction to mental futuring and pasting. Notice that ninety-nine percent of your fears are concerned with the stories you make up about what the future might hold for you. And most of the time these fears never come true. Yet you continue to create them, because that's all you know how to do.

The guilt we experience is always about the past. We do things the best we know how in any given moment and as we progress in knowledge, perhaps we would choose differently if we had it to do over. So why do we beat ourselves up because we didn't know how to do things differently in the past? The past is gone and there is nothing we can do to change it. But still we regret doing the best we knew how. The only thing that fearing an imaginary future or trying to fix a dead past does is destroy the joy and happiness we could experience in the present.

How many times have you worried that there just wouldn't be enough...of whatever enough was for you? Maybe you were worried that you couldn't pay the bills you had created. Maybe you could, maybe you couldn't, but how much good did it do you to worry about it? Or perhaps you have worried that your lover was cheating on you. Maybe he was, and maybe he wasn't. But did all of your worrying change anything?

The only thing that futuring and pasting does is block your intuition and your ability to receive the information that Love could share with you in the present. It saps your energy and the Life Force within you. Solutions to all problems are available, if you are open to receive them. Psychologists have demonstrated that the average human being's thoughts are focused on the present moment only three to five percent of the time. The rest of the time we're thinking about the future or the past. And we are so addicted to doing this that we aren't even conscious of doing it.

Learning to live in the present moment is perhaps the single most important thing one can ever learn to do. For in reality, NOW is all there is. All the pertinent information needed to live a productive, fulfilled life can be received in the present. Albert Einstein intuited the Theory of Relativity by being in the moment. He had a dream in which he saw a horse running across the universe on a beam of light. The next morning, as he was shaving, simply shaving and being in the moment, the meaning of his dream came to him. It took him ten years to put it down on paper, so others could understand, what he had intuited in the blinking of an eye.

No doubt you, too, have experienced powerful intuitive moments in your life. If you begin to pay attention, you will notice that they come when your mind is at rest. Just being in the present, not the least bit concerned with the future or the past. The reason you constantly engage in this futile act of futuring and pasting is that you are searching for answers to the problems in your life. You think that if you can find the answers, you can experience security and through security, happiness. You believe that if you can "figure out" your past and give it the proper "meaning" that you can somehow fix it. And you believe that if you can "figure out" the future you can control it. But it doesn't work that way and never will. You are just addicted to doing what you know how to do.

When I ask people in the workshops I hold what happiness is for them, the diversity of responses is staggering. What these answers have in common is that happiness is something that is largely missing from their lives; something that they don't have, something that they are looking for, something that lies outside of themselves. It only shows up momentarily and it can't be counted on. And for many, happiness is freedom from negative states; to be free from stress, tension, worry, doubt, pain, and poverty. Happiness, for many, is the absence of unhappiness.

In our consumer-oriented culture, success usually is equated with happiness. And success usually means financial success. The purpose of making money is to be able to buy the things that are supposed to bring us happiness. As long as we assume that happiness lies outside ourselves and that it can be purchased, it seems like common sense that we need to make money to buy happiness. And as long as we continue to assume this we will go on confusing happiness and fulfillment with the immediate gratification of our physical senses.

Let's take a closer look at what appears to be <u>common sense</u>. It may be <u>common</u>, but how much <u>sense</u> does it make? Common sense says that there is something wrong if you are not happy. You somehow have the right to expect to be happy. But you can't expect to be happy all the time. In a culture where anything can be bought, you assume that when you're not happy, you can buy and consume something that will bring you happiness. You go to a movie, go shopping, go out to dinner, buy a new car, change relationships, change jobs, move. The list is endless.

You think that to be happy, you must first do something you're not doing now, or have something you don't have now, or both. We can illustrate such common sense thinking as follows:

when I DO something (more, or better, or different)
then I can HAVE what I want
in order to BE happy.

When you experience the absence of happiness in your life, you simply take it for granted that what you're doing now isn't good enough, or it's the wrong thing to be doing. The conclusion you come to is that <u>as soon as</u> you have what you want, then you'll be happy. You believe the bumper sticker that reads, "He who dies with the most toys, wins." You think that real happiness lies outside of you somewhere in the future, and that <u>as soon as</u> you accumulate enough goodies, then you'll be happy.

Sometimes you change the order of your <u>common sense</u> around. You think that <u>if only</u> you were not doing what you're doing and things had been different in the past, then you'd have what you want and you'd be happy. That version of common sense looks like this:

when I HAVE enough (money, love, understanding)
then I can DO what I want
in order to BE happy

And so you plan and scheme, you regret what was, and hope for what will be. You daydream about as soon as and you wish that if only. And you spend most of your waking and dreaming hours regretting the past and hoping for the future.

> if only I had been loved as a child
> if only I'd been born rich
> if only I'd married someone else
> if only I had a different job
> if only I were better looking
> if only my life was more than it is, or better than it is,
>   or different from what it is

Or,

> as soon as I get that job
> as soon as I graduate and get my degree
> as soon as the kids are in school
> as soon as my spouse understands me better
> as soon as I get that promotion
> as soon as we get our own home
> as soon as my life is more than it is, or better than it is, or
> different from what it is.

The cruel irony is that the more time you spend experiencing yourself and your life in these ways, the more powerless you become, and the less happiness you experience. You can't go back in time and the future never gets here. So, regretting and hoping are a waste of time and energy. The time that's wasted is the present and the energy that's wasted is the power of fulfilling your human potential. The only time you can experience the power and vitality of life is in the present moment. The only time you can break through to your Higher Self and Love is right now.

Fulfilling and Forgiving

Happiness does not lie outside of yourself. It is not a condition absent from your life. To avoid the confusion associated with your common sense understanding of "happiness," let's talk about fulfillment instead. You were born into this world as material and spiritual being with potential and possibility. It is up to you to become a conscious human being, to fulfill your potential and possibility. A conscious human being is a human being fulfilling and forgiving itself. And the potential for being human is limitless. The possibility for your growth and development is unbounded.

The process of being, of fulfilling, of forgiving, and of sharing our beingness is the only process which ensures fulfillment. You have all the answers, all the resources you require to lead a fulfilling life. Trusting that truth may be difficult for you at times. But you were born as children naturally knowing that life works. Think of the characteristics of children. They're spontaneous and honest about their experience, their sensations, emotions, thoughts, intentions, and actions. When they're happy or angry, they express it. When they want to be held, they come and get a hug. When they're hungry, they let you know. They are very much in the moment. It is only after several years of programming that children learn how to be like adults and separate themselves from the presence of their emotional experience.

Natural Knowing

To live life fully and to be all that you already are, is to experience yourself in the process of fulfilling your human beingness. The only requirements are to trust your emotional experience and to express it honestly. The belief that in order to be happy you must do something in order to have something in order to be somebody or something is an illusion. Your only job as a human being is to BE. How you express your being in who you are and in what you do produces the natural conditions of living. Being is an expression of who you are. In being the expression of who you are in what you do, what you get to have as a natural consequence is your experience of yourself. The extent to which you're confused, unclear, and out of alignment about the purpose of life is the extent to which you're out of touch with your experience of yourself. You lose yourself in the quest for happiness if you assume that happiness lies outside of yourself. By assuming that you're not enough and that to be enough you first must do things outside of yourself, you lose yourself in the process of trying to find yourself. It's impossible to find yourself outside of yourself. You find your self in yourself. Consider the possibilities of living life from a state of being or natural knowing:

in BEING (who or what I am, in the present moment)
what I'm DOING (whatever it is)
I'm HAVING (the experience I want)

Being a human is an ongoing, never-ending process. A human being isn't somebody or something. Being human is a process of fulfillment and forgiving, of being conscious, of realizing our possibilities, of embracing our power, of acting in the unfolding moment. If you get confused and act as if your self is a thing with static boundaries, if you act as if you are a set of relatively unchanging characteristics, you are bound to experience yourself as being in conflict with others and with life. You will experience yourself at war.

Socrates is given credit for having said that the unexamined life is not worth living. Most of us are frightened at the prospect of examining our lives. We are afraid that we might not be the images we have pretended to be. We are afraid that if we are not our bounded egos we may not know who we are.

What would it mean to be a process of fulfillment and forgiveness rather than a product of your environment or an image of an identity? It seems safer and easier, at least in the short run, to look for something that doesn't exist, in places where you can never find it. Your self isn't in the past or the future, and it's not a neatly defined identity. It's a process of being. And all that your self is will still be there after the images have gone. Most of us look for what we don't have in places that are familiar, but the search doesn't produce the results we are looking for. We all carry our own Light, we already have our own answers. To go looking for what we assume we don't have is a double illusion. Ultimately, it's life threatening to ourselves and to the planet.

Content and Context

Another way to talk about this and to compare <u>common sense</u> with <u>natural knowing,</u> is to say that from the point of view of common sense, each of us lives in a variety of contexts. As such, you are a content, a "thing" within larger contexts. Contexts are relationships, families, groups, organizations, societies, cultures, and the planet. But what if you experience yourself, not as a content, not as an object, but as a context, a process? That is the truth of natural knowing. You are not an object among other objects. You are a context of being, a context of possibility and potential. You are a context of growth and development. You are not a content whose identity can be completely known and whose characteristics are fixed and unchanging. You are a process. You are in the process of fulfilling yourself as a human being. You are becoming more conscious, more fulfilling, more forgiving. And as you become more conscious, the context of your experience of yourself becomes ever larger.

From a common sense perspective, you assume the context of your life is relatively stable and fixed. Where you assume you have freedom or power is in the contents you choose to put into the context of your life. For example, you can assume that you can buy different things to put in the context of your life that will change your life. If you remain focused at the content level, your emphasis is on doing what it takes to have what you want. The condition of natural knowing is fundamentally different. Rather than assuming that you are a content in a larger context, you experience yourself as a <u>context of being</u>. There is a paradox here. The way you become more conscious, more fulfilled, more of who you are is by being conscious, fulfilled, and who you are right now, in this moment.

Fulfillment is a natural state of being and knowing. Picture it as a field that engulfs you. Much of the time you're not conscious of its presence. When you are consciously <u>being</u>, you know satisfaction, you have the sense of fulfillment. You feel secure, warm, and safe in the moment. In that moment what you want to be doing in order to have what you want will become apparent.

Start paying attention to how your mind is constantly running back and forth from the future to the past...from the fear and hope of the future to the guilt and regret of the past. By becoming more aware of this process of mental oscillation, you can begin to focus more fully on the present and begin more and more to actually experience the fulfillment that living in the present can bring. As you do, what you desire will begin to create itself increasingly in the present. It is almost as if you can warp time and space. And you will begin to experience less fear, greater power, more joy and an abundance of intuitive insight.

As you become more aligned with the present, you will become more sensitive to your feelings. Thoughts and ideas will come to you that can change your life. Perhaps it will be an idea for a new invention, or a new business endeavor. And the ways and means to accomplish your desires will come to you, also.

As you begin to receive this information, act on it. The only time action can take place is in the present. Don't trust in your fears any longer. Act on your feelings and intuition.

Now, of course, you can learn from the past and plan future courses of action, but the learning and planning can only be done in the present. As you learn to ask your Higher Self what it is you should be doing with your life, if you listen, you will receive answers. Then act on them. Begin by beginning. The journey of a thousand miles begins by taking the first step. Perhaps you feel the need to be a better parent and someone tells you about a good book they have just read on parenting. Read it. It wasn't by accident or coincidence you were told about the book. There are no accidents in the Universe. Or perhaps someone compliments you on a certain talent you possess. Develop the talent. And be patient with yourself. It's taken years to develop this addictive pattern of running to the future and back to the past. And it will take some time to learn how to live in the present. But you can learn to do it. It's not something you need to fight or struggle with. It's more of a relaxing into the present than a struggling out of the past and future. Your mind was originally con-structed to live in the present and wants to do so naturally. Be patient with yourself and love yourself as you learn to live more fully in the Eternal Now. Why worry so incessantly about your life? Are your problems really that serious? Maybe they just repossessed your car. Big deal! You can get another one. You got the first one didn't you? Cease thinking about tomorrow; what you will eat, what you will drink or what you will wear. Is not life more than matter, and your body more than clothing? Look at the birds in the air; they don't plant or harvest or gather food for storage, yet Love feeds them. And aren't you of much greater awareness than they? Can any of you extend your life for even one hour by your incessant worrying? Life is not to be governed by many thoughts, but thoughts are to be directed and guided by Love. "Ask, and you will receive; seek and you shall find; knock and the door will be opened."

CONQUERING YOUR FEARS

Only beauty surrounds me.

There is nothing to fear.

I am eternal.

Fear is an illusion.

I am love.

Love was and is the original emotion ever felt throughout the Universe. God is Love. Love is the beginning and the end, the Alpha and Omega. And It will be forever. Experiencing Love and the Truth it has to offer was the original design of our experience. If we took away all of the fear and anxiety from our lives, the only thing left would be Love and Truth. Love and Truth are the natural state of human beingness. We were created to be in alignment with Love and Truth, and to be channels of receptivity to these subtle Universal forces. But at some point in our conscious development we conceived ourselves to be isolated, individuated and alone... apart and separated from Love, Truth, God, Goddess, All That Is. At that moment we blocked the Love, disrupted this Universal alignment, and experienced the opposing force of Love in the Universe, fear. And instead of using that fear to turn us back and align ourselves once again with Love, we began to believe that fear was the truth of our experience and we began to trust in fear rather than Love. Fear is the most destructive force in our lives. Trust in fear has been the cause of all of the pain and suffering in the world. And the cruel irony is that we create our fears by denying Love. What has followed has been a downward spiral, deeper and deeper into a relatively unconscious existence on this material plane. This is what man and religion have called the fall; being kicked out of the garden, committing the original sin. The confusion and myth, created to explain this simple process have had men bickering amongst one another for centuries.

The original fear is the fear of loneliness. The fear that you are all alone, cut off from God. All other fears have originated from this primary fear. Anxiety, frustration, worry, guilt, anger, jealousy and hate are but thinly veiled expressions of this fear. And if we fail to see them as such, the consequences can be devastating.

So let us discuss fear and learn how to overcome it so that we might once again return to our natural state of being. A state in which we place our trust in Love, rather than in fear.

The Positive Side of Fear

First, let us discuss the positive aspects of fear, for as an emotion, it does have a purpose. I have found four ways in which fear can be helpful, if understood properly. First, it can be a whisper to us that we are in physical danger. For example, if we step off a curb into the path of an oncoming semi, we had better experience enough fear to get out of its way. Fear can alert us to impending danger or physical harm that might injure us biologically.

Secondly, fear can slow us down. It can cause us to put on the brakes.

When we are entering unknown territory, perhaps in the form of a new relationship or a business venture, fear can whisper to us saying, "There is something you are missing here, or there is something you don't understand. Slow down. Be patient. Stop, look, and listen before you proceed any further." By learning to listen to these promptings, we can get in touch with our intuitive Higher Self and avoid a great many painful lessons in life. But to learn this you must become better acquainted with your emotional world. If you feel uncomfortable about anything, pay attention to your feelings. Perhaps a friend makes a request that you don't feel good about, but you don't know why you are feeling this uneasiness. Love has shown me that there is a always a reason for feeling what I feel. Slow down until you know and understand your feelings.

Thirdly, fear can teach us where we lack trust. This is usually a lack of trust in ourselves or in our own abilities, but it can be a warning that we are trusting in someone or something naively. For example, someone very close to you might tell you that they care for you deeply, but you have a hard time believing it. If they have consistently shown love towards you in both word and deed, why don't you trust what they are telling you? In such a situation, your fear is trying to show you that you need to work on trusting more in your own self worth and perhaps finding ways to love and accept yourself more fully, as the other person accepts you. If, on the other hand, this person is telling you that they care deeply for you, but has constantly demonstrated otherwise by cheating on you, criticizing you in front of others, taking advantage of you, etc., your fear could be trying to tell you that you trust naively and need to back up and get a broader perspective of your reality.

Finally, fear can show us when we are working with a faulty belief system. In the previous example the consistently loving person expresses their love for you and you feel a little distrustful. Why? Perhaps you are living your life based on an old belief or map that says, "I'm not lovable, so you can't love me. And I know you can't, because no one has loved me in the past." Or, "I know you say you love me, but if you loved me, you'd never leave me, and I know you will someday because everyone else has in the past." If you don't reprogram your mind, your bio-computer, with an accurate map of your present reality, (i.e. this person does love me and has shown me love consistently time and time again, therefore, I am lovable) you'll repeat your past and recreate the very thing you fear the most, abandonment and loneliness. The need to be right about our unconscious or core beliefs is the overriding programming in just about all of our lives. If you believe you're not lovable, and you need to be right about your belief, you will go to any length to prove that you aren't lovable. Even if it means you have to self destruct in a healthy, loving relationship. Trust me, I know, because I've done it in the past, before I understood how powerful I really was, and before I ever knew what a belief system looked like.

These are four areas in which fear can be used as an ally to serve you rather than enslave you. So fear does have a positive side. But what about its negative side? This must be examined so you can understand why fear can be so devastating in your life, and why you are so afraid to look at your fears. It is difficult to make this examination because most of us have so many fears that the very thought of dealing with them scares us to death. I have found this to be so in my life; I know how difficult it is to confront your fears. But I also know that the only way to be free of your fears is to examine them and work through them. There is no other way.

Looking at the Downside of Fear

There are seven major reasons why fear can be so devastating. First, fear separates you from you. Once fear has engulfed you it separates you from the thoughts, and feelings of your Higher Self. After cutting you off from your True Self, it can separate you from your reality and the knowledge that you create your reality.

Do you realize that many people will fight with you and argue to no end, if you tell them that they create their own reality. Do you have any idea how fearful people are who deny that they create their own reality? Why they are brimming with fear. It has cut them entirely off from themselves and the Truth of their reality. They are lost in fear and all the while denying that they have any fear. Fear has engulfed them to the point that they can't even recognize fear as fear. They are not evil or bad, they are simply lost. This does not mean that you should embrace them or invite them into your lives. Nor does it mean that you should despise them. Simply see that they are lost and the greatest thing you can do for such people, and the world, is to conquer and overcome your own fears, thereby freeing up the flow of Love and increasing the Love in your own life, your own reality. As you do this, the Love that emanates from you as you go about your daily lives will have a much greater influence on those lost in fear than any other thing you could possibly do. Trying to make them see things your way will only frighten them more, and cause greater conflict in their lives. Besides you already have all you can handle to work on conquering your own fears. You don't need to shoulder the burdens and fears of the entire world. You came here to create heaven on earth. You came here to bring Love to this material plane and the way to do that most effectively is to make your reality a reality of Love and Peace.

Secondly, after separating you from you and your reality, fear paralyzes you. It can enslave you and place you in a state in which you are unable to act. It holds you in your insecurities, jealousies, doubts, and anger. It can actually cripple you. You might ask, "Can just a tiny fear paralyze me?" No, a tiny fear will only numb you, but as your fears grow and multiply the deadening, numbing effect can turn to paralysis. For paralysis is simply numbing to the point of no longer being able to feel. Power is the ability to act, but when fear has overcome you, you lose your power and can no longer act to bring about your dreams and desires.

How many times in your life have you wanted something better or more or different, but were afraid that you couldn't have it, so you didn't even try to achieve your goal or dream? How many times have you heard other people talk about wanting a new job, more money, a nicer home, a better relationship, etc., but were too afraid to go after it? They say things like:

"I'm not that lucky."
"I'm not smart enough."
"I don't have the proper education."
"I'm overtrained for the job."
"I'm undertrained for the job."
"I'm too old."
"It's just too late."

What they're really saying is that they are afraid to try because they are afraid they might fail. Or they are afraid of success and their ability to deal with it. So they remain in their paralysis and in their mediocrity. It is easier to go on doing what they know how to do than to face their fears about changing what has become so familiar to them. Their fears remain and their dreams are never realized, simply because they are too afraid to confront their fears and overcome them.

Thirdly, fear perpetuates the past. What is it that you are most afraid of? Is it not the past repeating itself? And why? Because it has done so before. You're afraid that your lover or companion will leave you, because others have left you in the past. You're afraid that no one loves you, because no one has loved you in the past. You're afraid that things won't turn out the way you want them to, because they haven't in the past. And your fear of the past repeating itself actually holds you in your past and is the very reason your past seems to repeat itself over and over again. Are your past experiences really comprehensive enough to define clearly or to give accurate meaning to your present experience? NO! So why do you cling to them and search your past for answers to your present experience? Only Love and Truth can supply the information necessary to navigate successfully through your present situation. Only through trusting in Love will your life work in appropriate ways. You have been trusting in fear for ages and what have the results been? Trusting in fear brings confusion and pain. Trusting in Love brings Light and Joy.

But there are payoffs for continuing to trust in your fears. There are reasons you hold onto your fears. If you conquer your fears and get your life together, who's going to pay attention to you? In the past it has always been the squeaky wheels that got the grease. It has always been those with the greatest problems who seem to get the most attention. The victims are the ones who need someone to rescue them. But there are prices to pay for the payoffs of continuing to trust in fear. And the payoffs are not worth the prices in pain and resentment you have to pay for an unfulfilled life and dreams never realized. But like any good addict you want the payoffs you get from trusting in fear more than the fulfillment which comes from trusting in Love, because that's all you know.

Fourthly, fear can be very addictive. Notice what happens the next time you wake up in the morning and feel just great. Everything is wonderful! You're going through your day and nothing is wrong. Then all of a sudden you just can't stand it any longer. There is simply nothing bothering you, nothing making you anxious or worried, and it drives you crazy. You don't know how to make it through the day without getting a fix. You're a fear junkie so you make things up to worry about. You have a checklist of fears, so you begin running down your list.

You're afraid you'll miss an appointment or screw up at your job.
You're afraid your lover is going to leave you, or
that you'll never find anyone to love.
You're afraid someone is going to hurt you.
You're afraid you aren't going to have enough money to pay the
bills you've created.
You're afraid your children aren't going to turn out the way you
had always hoped they would.
And your afraid that no matter what you do, things are going to get
worse.

Your list goes on and on. You have no idea what it would be like to live without fear. And you deny that you create your fears. You keep telling yourself that they're real. You're afraid that if you don't worry about your future, there just won't be any future. Everything will fall apart and your life will be ruined. But it won't. You're just an addict looking for another excuse to get a fix. You get tired and probably need a nap, but you take a hit of fear instead to get going. And you don't even see it. You have become addicted to fear.

Fifthly, fear accommodates all of your manipulations and the games you play with yourself and others. By trusting in fear you justify all of your game playing. You get to hurt people because you're scared. You say things like, "Well, I hurt you because I didn't think you loved me." And your companion responds with, "Oh, I guess I can stop bleeding now. You only hurt me because you were scared. I get it." You think that your fear justifies your inappropriate actions. It doesn't. You trash people and ridicule them in front of their friends because you are afraid they don't like you. And you do it because you say you're scared. Wake up. You're engulfed in fear.

Sixthly, fear fuels your blockages. You're afraid you won't succeed and the more you listen to your fear, that great teller of lies, the more you believe in what it is saying to you. If you believe in fear, you will experience more and more of it. And you will get to be right about your beliefs, rather than succeed at reaching your dreams and goals in life.

Finally, fear separates you from Love, or God. This separation will eventually cause you to deny Love and its existence. And once separated from Love, you lose touch with yourself and your true identity as an eternal Being of Light and Love. If you had listened to the fear in the first place, it could have warned you to put on the brakes and turn back. Your original fear, the fear of loneliness, the fear of being separated from God, could have helped you back on the road to living a life guided by and filled with Love. But fear has now swallowed you up and you are lost.

Observe the reality we have collectivly created by trusting in fear. We have built 50,000 to 75,000 nuclear warheads based on our fears of what might happen in the future. And by building them, by assuming that our fear of the future is reality, we have actually created the reality motivated by our fears in the first place.

Observe the hunger and starvation throughout the world. Would anyone be starving on this planet if we weren't worried or fearful about not having enough food for tomorrow? We are afraid there isn't enough food to go around so we hoard food in cans, cellars, grain elevators and government warehouses. Food rots in the First World, while people starve in the Third World (and think of the insanity of distinctions such as First, Second and Third World, as if we weren't all in this together interdependently). We believe that it doesn't make economic sense to feed the world, even when the food is available. So we complulsively create the conditions under which our assumptions of scarcity are validated. That people are starving becomes evidence that we don't have enough food, and the reason for the necessity of hoarding it at the same time. It is a negative-loop cycle. A doomed self-fulfilling prophecy. By assuming that your fears are real, you build your reality on the foundation of your fears. And the reality you create justifies your fear. Your fear then necessitates the insanity of your defensive behaviour, whether in interpersonal relationships or in international relations. And the more you do it the more real it seems. Your fears are your worst enemies. But you continue to invite them into your daily lives, by assuming that they are real. By assuming that your fears are real, you make them real. You real-<u>ize</u> them. And as you realize them in your life, they count as evidence for the truth of your fear in the first place. You assume that being afraid and being confused are simply part of being alive. And in that assumption you become completely lost.

As a child perhaps you were afraid of the dark. Remember how you would enter a dark room and create all sorts of fearful nightmares allowing your fear to express itself! When you could no longer stand the fear you reached out and turned on the light. What happened to the nightmares when the darkness vanished? What happened to your fear? <u>Do you see that fear is an illusion</u>? Only Love is real.

So isn't it time to conquer your fears? Are you ready to enjoy all the Love and Happiness you were meant to enjoy? You can if you choose to. To start, simply forgive yourself. Forgive yourself for becoming lost in fear. It's okay. In fact, you did it so that you could grow in understanding and knowledge. That's the symbolism in the garden when Adam and Eve chose to eat of the fruit of the knowledge of good and evil. By exercising your free will and choosing to come to this material plane of existence you separated yourself from the presence of Love so you could learn for yourself the difference between Love and fear, the difference between what works and what doesn't work. And now that you have learned that trusting in fear doesn't work, you can again exercise your free will and place your trust in Love. But this time you do so consciously. You return to God, you find your way back home because that's where you choose to be. You can now return to the presence of Love and Truth, knowing that you are loved and that your life does have meaning and purpose. And it is Love which can share that purpose with you and help you create a fulfilling and satisfying life.

Transformation
The transformation is a simple one. Don't make it into something of

great complexity. Begin by forgiving yourself and become aware of your fears, your anxieties and worries. The next time you feel afraid of something, confront it. Examine your life and track your fear like a hunter stalking his prey. Ask yourself, "What is it that I'm afraid of?" An interesting think will happen. As soon as you become curious about the fear, as you define it, name it, treat it as an object, and examine it, you will gain insight into yourself. This alone will create a great space for Love to fill the illusory emptiness you have created within yourself by trusting in fear. As you do, ask Love for guidance. Ask Love what your fears are about. And learn to listen in that quiet place within; your heart of hearts. Answers will come. Be aware. Be attentive. Listen. Be sensitive and be conscious of the Love working in your life.

Here is an exercise that can help you in conquering your fears. Go somewhere where you will not be disturbed for 20 or 30 minutes. Perhaps your bedroom, living room, or some place in nature. A place where the phone won't ring, where your spouse or children won't disturb you, where you can be all by yourself. Once you are there, sit in a comfortable position and relax. Notice your body and how it feels. Notice your thoughts and feelings. Notice your surroundings.   And relax. Now, pick a fear. Any fear will do, but perhaps you would like to pick your greatest fear, whatever that might be for you. Perhaps you are afraid that your lover might leave you, or maybe you are scared to death of flying or heights...whatever it may be. Now close your eyes and envision your greatest fear coming to pass. Don't be afraid that by envisioning your fear that you will actually create its happening. Intent produces results, and your intent is to conquer your fear, not to bring it to pass.

As you envision this fear, what is the worst possible outcome you can imagine? See it in its entirety. What's the worst thing that could happen if this fear were to manifest itself in your life? Do you see it? Can you imagine actually living through it? And if this were to happen, what is the worst possible thing that could happen after its occurrence? Play the whole thing out in its entirety. After you have done this, embrace your fear. Experience it, acknowledge it, and then watch it dissolve and disappear. It is only an illusion. An illusion that you have created because fear is what you know how to create. You are addicted to having fear in your life. But you can overcome it and conquer it. There is nothing that you cannot work through and solve. And now you know this to be true. Then open your eyes and forgive yourself once again. Acknowledge your fearlessness for having envisioned and overcome your fear. Then love yourself. Accept yourself just as you are. You are perfect! Jesus said, "Be ye therefore perfect even as your Father which is in heaven is perfect." Do you think that He would have asked you to do this if it were impossible? If you think that perfection is some static, unchanging state of existence where your days are spent flying around in the clouds playing a harp, then you're right. This imagined perfection is impossible to attain, because it doesn't exist. When does a flower as it is growing become perfect? When does a child in its growth and development become perfect...or lose its perfection? They are perfect from day one, just as you are. This doesn't mean that there isn't more that you can become, but as a process of becoming, you are already perfect. You are a perfect creation of Love that Love cares for so deeply and fully that words cannot express the profundity of that Love. And everything in your life is perfect. It is perfect for your growth and development. As you work with your fears and learn how to use them in appropriate ways, ways that benefit and serve you, rather than being enslaved by them, you will notice more and more Love in your life. It has always been there, but because you have trusted in fear more than Love, you just didn't notice it. And as you begin to trust more in Love, Love will engulf you and dispel all of your fears. You can begin today to live a life filled with Love. The choice is yours.

MASTERING YOUR
FEELINGS

I observe my emotions.

I allow.

I accept.

To live is to feel.

I live to love.

When's the last time you had an argument with someone you love dearly? Maybe it was a little disagreement, or perhaps an all-out screaming match. Or possibly you're the type who lashes out by refusing to communicate. Someone did something that you didn't like and you're going to show them who's boss. So you don't talk to them for a few days, or a week, or longer. You're right, they're wrong, and you're going to prove it. And this person gets to experience rejection, emotional and perhaps physical abandonment and a great deal of pain. But are you really happy by acting this way? You lose, they lose, you hurt, they hurt, and nobody wins. And if these misguided attempts to punish continue long enough, the love you share might even be destroyed. Then you can go out and start over with someone who <u>really</u> understands you. Or if it's one of your children, maybe they can move out and you don't have to see one another or talk to one another anymore. Isn't it wonderful living under such conditions? You get to experience pain, anger, loneliness and if it gets bad enough, maybe you can become a drunk or drug addict or end up in therapy. Maybe you could even decide to end it all and commit suicide.

Or maybe the pain will become so intense that you'll begin to wake up. What doesn't work, doesn't work. For years I spent my life in relationships that didn't work and always ended in failure because I refused to learn to understand and process my feelings. My feelings scared me to death and rather than face them and find out what they were all about, I spent my time in stinking taverns, talking with drunks about how rotten life was. It didn't work for 33 years and if it wasn't for Love intervening in my life, I might have never learned why it didn't work. But there are ways of dealing with your feelings that work. And once you learn to process your thoughts and emotions appropriately you can have it all. All of the love, all of the intimacy and passion, all of the warmth and sharing for which you have been searching. But not until you see and understand that no one is doing anything emotionally to you; you are doing it to yourself. You are the creator of your reality and your reality is nothing more or less than the world you create with your thoughts and emotions, your beliefs and assumptions. In fact, your thoughts and emotions are the only things you have any control over at all. If you think you have control over anything else, you're dreaming. It's simply a story you have made up to give yourself some imagined, false sense of security. But once you realize that you are the creator of your world by believing what you choose to believe and feeling what you choose to feel, you can transcend this world of pain and suffering and bring Heaven and Love into your life once and for all.

Emotions

So let's talk about your feelings, your emotions. I'm going to define emotions as negative or positive, but in a slightly different way than we have commonly defined negative and positive. <u>Any emotion, pleasant or unpleasant, that is repressed, and not expressed, by experiencing it, is a negative emotion. Any emotion, pleasant or unpleasant that is expressed by experiencing it, is a positive emotion</u>. This means that no matter what you are feeling at any given moment it is an appropriate emotion. You are feeling it; acknowledge the truth of your experience. It's okay because you are okay. It's perfect because you are perfect. The situations in life which we call problems arise because we don't understand how to process, express or handle our emotions in appropriate, productive ways. When you experience any emotion and acknowledge your feelings, you can learn to process that emotion. By expressing it appropriately, like magic it will dissipate and go away. And by expressing it I don't mean projecting it onto another person. If you are experiencing anger, experience it, feel it, become curious about your experience and the emotion will dissolve. Don't take it out on those around you. Just experience it. Taking your anger out on others will do nothing but bump out everybody, including yourself. <u>The most important thing you can ever do for other people is to leave them feeling better emotionally after being in your presence</u>.

Any emotion that is repressed will continue to exist and seek expression or manifestation in whatever way it can. Unexpressed emotions are what cause most of our physical ailments. Headaches and ulcers are created by attempting to bury your feelings rather than expressing them by experiencing them. And after a time, if you repeatedly avoid processing your emotions, neurosis will set in and an unbelievable state of confusion will be created. At this point you will become so confused that you no longer have any idea what you are feeling and at times may become unable to feel at all. The results can be devastating. By learning to handle and express your emotions appropriately, a great deal of pain and suffering can be avoided. There are many types of healing that can occur in our lives. We can heal our bodies by exercising and eating more nutritional foods and this is important. <u>But the most crucial healing that anyone can experience is emotional healing</u>. Once you have healed yourself emotionally, everything else in your life will fall into place.

Most of us get along just fine with pleasant emotions. When we feel loved, happy, trusted, cared for, etc., life just seems to flow. It's the unpleasant ones that most of us have difficulty with. So let's talk about those.

When It Hurts

Hurt is perhaps the most difficult, unpleasant emotion any of us have to experience. If we were totally conscious human beings, we would realize that nothing can hurt us but our faulty belief systems and addictive behavior patterns. In other words, <u>we are the only ones who can hurt us and we do so by setting up unrealistic illusions or expectations about the way things are or should be rather than accepting what is</u>. But until we have reached complete consciousness we are where we are and should not beat ourselves up or be unloving towards ourselves because we are not yet something else.

Coming to consciousness is an ongoing process and along the way we are going to experience a wide range of emotions. Learning to process these emotions in appropriate ways will only speed up our progress. Doing what works, really works.

When we lose something that we mistakenly thought was ours in the first place, we can experience hurt and pain. When we lose something or someone we love, it can hurt very badly. When we lose our self-esteem, or our sense of self-worth, it hurts. When we lose our illusionary control over some aspect of our lives, it hurts. When expectations that we have created are not met, it hurts. And hurt, if not expressed at the moment we experience it, turns into anger. And anger does not age well. It festers and becomes bitter with age. The longer we hold the hurt in, the angrier we become and the more pain we experience.

I once had an hour-long screaming match with Erin because she forgot to leave the keys where she had promised to leave them. I was consequently late for an appointment. We fought and screamed and hurt one another, when all we really wanted to do was love one another. But neither of us knew how to process our emotions at the time. We had been hurting and not expressing the hurt for a year and a half. And the hurt had turned into anger and we didn't understand what was happening until it was too late.

Love has since taught me a great deal about processing my emotions. When someone does something that hurts you, express the hurt the moment it happens. Don't get angry and project the hurt onto the other person inappropriately. Instead talk through it with the other person. Experience the pain and simply begin to talk out loud to yourself and let the other person witness your pain. Let your eyes get watery and tell them, "It hurts to know that you are having an affair with another person." Or, "It hurts because you just wrecked my car and don't really seem too concerned." Or, "It hurts when you scream at me because I love you."

Just talk to yourself out loud and let them experience your pain. If a person refuses to hear and listen to your pain, they don't love you, probably because they don't know a great deal about loving, and you don't need them in your life. They might change, in time, but if they have hurt you and refuse to hear your pain, you had better get out of their way, because I promise you, they will hurt you again.

Taking Care of Yourself

It is your responsibility to look out for yourself and defend yourself. No one else will. And there are only two reasons you should ever accept from another as to why they have hurt you. They could come up with a thousand different reasons to justify their actions, but the only two you should accept are: One, they meant to hurt you; or two, they were unthinking. The reason you must take such a stand and tell them this is to bring them to a higher level of consciousness. Then give them room to think about their actions and their feelings towards you. Allow them the chance to grow and allow yourself the same opportunity.

If you don't experience your pain and hurt the moment it happens, your only other recourse is repression. And repressed pain will turn into anger and resentment and eventually find expression at a later date. Chances are that when that day comes it won't be pleasant.

If the person who has hurt you listens to your pain, the relationship will be stronger for it. Your love and concern for one another will grow. But if a person refuses to hear it, get out of their way and ask yourself why you have attracted such a person into your life. Figure out what it was that you wanted them to teach you about you, and get on with it. Learn the lesson and get on with life. Let go and head down river. Use the experience as an opportunity to grow and learn to love yourself better.

By learning to process your pain in appropriate ways in the present, it will never become anger and resentment.

Dealing with Your Childhood

As I began to observe my life experience more carefully, I found that I had been carrying around a lot of hurt, anger and resentment from my childhood. For years I was angry at my mother and father, and blamed them for my problems as an adult. And much of the time I wasn't even aware that I was doing it. I had repressed almost all of the painful emotions from my childhood. And as an adult I was paying the penalty, along with a great deal of interest, for not having processed these old emotions.

Love finally taught me that all relationships need to be completed. They need to be resolved. If your source relationships with your parents have never been completed or resolved within yourself, you will never be able have a healthy relationship with someone else. If the source relationship with your mother was never resolved, every relationship you have with another woman will be a relationship with your mother, whether you are conscious of it or not. If you haven't resolved the source relationship with your father, every relationship you have with another man will be a relationship with your father. For years of my adult life, it was as though I was walking around wearing a pair of dark glasses. Every relationship I had with a woman was a relationship in which I was seeking the nurturing and bonding I never received from my mother. The woman didn't look like my mother, but the tint in my dark glasses held an image of my mother, and I was unconsciously projecting her onto them. I then recreated my past relationship with my mother, without ever realizing it.

My mother was in her early twenties when the problems in her marriage began. I was a small child and had no idea what it meant for a woman to be married to an alcoholic who was having affairs with other women and justified his actions to the point of using violence. Think of the pain and hurt she was experiencing! I was too small to understand any of this. All I knew was that she wasn't paying a great deal of attention to me. Nor was my father. So I began to throw temper tantrums and fight with her to gain her attention. As I grew older I began to drink, smoke, and use drugs, which certainly got her attention because of her religious beliefs. I thought that I was the cause of the anger and pain in her life. Twenty years later I was unconsciously recreating the same type of relationships with first my wife, and again with Erin. I was still throwing temper tantrums, smoking, drinking, and taking drugs and I don't need to tell you that I was not a real joy to live with. And I was completely unaware that I was behaving this way simply because I had never resolved the source relationship with my mother. My mother had become Eve in the garden; she represented all other women in the world to me.

In my late twenties I resolved my relationship with my father, without knowing what I had done. But I am still working on resolving the relationship with my mother. And I know that I am near completion, because I now have some wonderful relationships with women.

In the Bible, Isaiah and Paul talk about the "forgetting of former things" and Jesus talked about how He had come to turn father against son and mother against daughter, etc. I have come to see that they were talking about leaving home, about letting go of the the past and resolving your source relationships, through forgiveness and understanding. "Let the dead bury their dead." If you are ever going to have healthy, nurturing relationships in your adult life, you will need to complete your source relationships. To do that you need to process all of the old emotional hurt and anger you have been carrying around with you about your parents, and perhaps your grandparents. So let me share some things that have worked for me.

Processing Repressed Anger

First, as I mentioned before, write out everything you remember about your childhood. Put down on paper all of the painful memories that you have tried so hard to repress. And take your time. Get it all out. Let all of that old repressed anger surface. Then feel it, experience it, let it engulf you. Remember, negative emotions are emotions that have never been expressed, so get them out. Express them! Experience them! I know this might sound terrifying, but once again, life is paradoxical. The only way out is through. You will find that if you experience these emotions and let them engulf you, they will dissolve. By holding them in, you are simply blocking the natural flow of the Love you were meant to experience.

Once you have done this, if your parents are still alive, go and talk with them about your pain. Again, don't vent your anger at them, but talk through it by talking out loud to yourself and letting them experience, or be witness, to your pain. Complete the relationship and forgive them. They had no idea what they were doing. Let it go and get on with your life.

If they won't hear your pain, or perhaps if they have passed on, write them a letter. And take a long time writing it. Polish the letter and make sure you have said exactly what you want to say. Then, if they are still alive, mail the letter to them. If they are dead, go to the gravesite and read the letter out loud. I then suggest you tear the letter up and burn it. Spread the ashes over the gravesite or throw them into the sea or a river or flush them down the toilet. This may sound morbid, but it works. Do it. Get rid of the pain, the anger and resentment once and for all. Let it go and grow.

Or you can choose not to resolve these relationships, and continue through life repeating your past like a good addict. You can continue to experience the pain, guilt and depression, of your childhood, or choose to deal with it once and for all. Once you do, you will be free to live a life filled with Love. "For you shall know the Truth, and the Truth shall set you free."

Deal with your repressed feelings. Handle them and release yourself from the past. I promise that as you begin to clear these blockages from your life and spirit, the energy and Love that will begin to flow through you will seem miraculous and beyond your wildest dreams. Allow Love into your life. "Physician, heal thyself."

USING YOUR WORLD
AS A MIRROR

In everyone I see God.

Love and beauty surround me.

I experience good in all.

I learn without resistance.

I embrace change.

Let us discuss two principles of life. They are both aspects of subtle physics. The first principle Love has shown me is that the Universe is holographic. One of the aspects of a hologram is that the whole is manifested in the part and the part is a manifestation, a projection or reflection of the whole. The second principle is that our experiences in life come about through, or are caused by, the Law of Attraction. Light is attracted to Light. Intelligence is attracted to intelligence. And Love is attracted to Love. You are not simply the matter which you call your body, but also the energy force which attracts the matter of your physical body into its present form. You are the Source of your Life and its co-creator, working in or out of alignment with your Creator, at any given moment. Your outer reality is a reflection of your inner reality. Gandhi taught that, "The more efficient a force is the more silent and the more subtle it is. Love is the subtlest force in the world." The laws and principles which govern and influence our lives are very subtle and can only be understood by the patient observer and the astute listener. The answers to life which we all seek are manifest in our physical reality, but to perceive them for what they are we must go within and consult our inner voice, the Source of all Knowing.

Learning to Pay Attention

If you want to see yourself, take a look at the world you have created for yourself. For example, there were times in my life when financially I was doing very well, but my relationships with my wife or companion were unbearable. All of my friends were in similar situations. I was surrounded by millionaires living impoverished emotional and spiritual lives. But I didn't see that they were simply a reflection of me. I had actually attracted them to me to show me to me, and didn't understand what I had done. I didn't understand mirroring and the only thing I knew about holograms was that they were the little designs on my credit cards. I always thought that my friends were the ones with problems. I didn't realize that they were reflections of me. Since then Love has shown me the truth of my experience.

Who are your friends? Who are the people closest to you? What are they doing with their lives? What are their problems? What are their strengths? Why have you attracted them into your life? What are their lives saying about you? Is it possible that they are simply a projection of you? I believe that if you are honest with yourself, you will find that this is exactly what they are.

Are your relationships working? Are your friends' relationships working? Do you enjoy your present occupation? Do your friends enjoy theirs? Are you a constant fault finder? Are your friends fault finders?

Are you overweight? Are your friends overweight? Do you wish you had more money? Do your friends feel the same way? And you thought it was just coincidence that you and your friends are so much alike. Do you have any idea how powerful you are? You have created your life and your reality to teach you more about you. Do you get it? Their addictions are your addictions. Their strengths are your strengths. Their weaknesses are your weaknesses. Do you understand?

Relationships and Growth

Carl Jung explained this process in part by pointing out how we use projection, or mirroring, in our relationships. Jung theorized that within each psyche there exists a contrasexual archetype. If you are male, your female aspect, or archetype, is the anima. If you are female, your male energy is referred to as the animus. When we "fall in love" we project our contrasexual energy onto the object of our love. If we understand the process, we are then able to visualize and understand our own selves better by using the other individual as our mirror.

In my relationship with Erin I had projected my anima, my female energy, onto her. When I asked for her advise, which wasn't very often, everything she told me to do was identical to what my inner female was instructing me to do. But I didn't always act on what the Universe and Love were sharing with me because I didn't understand what was taking place. She told me not to do drugs, drink alcohol, smoke cigarettes, or focus my life entirely on sex. When I asked my inner voice what I should do with my life, the same instructions were given. But I was simply too lazy to do what she was telling me, and what I was telling myself. And I had become so addicted to these behavioral patterns in my search for a pseudo-spiritual experience, that when I finally did begin to take control of my life rather than simply talk about it, too much damage had been done to save the relationship. And we were both choosing different paths.

By learning to use your world as a mirror, it is very easy to find the areas in your life where you need to work to bring yourself to a greater degree of consciousness. If I had used Erin's confusion about what she wanted to do with her life as a key to my own world of confusion concerning career choices, I could have avoided a great amount of stress, pain, and financial loss. But I didn't understand mirroring at the time. I didn't understand that she was mirroring my own inner confusion.

As I reflect more deeply on the relationship with this woman, I am now able to embrace that we were perfect teachers for one another. Erin was extremely lazy. So was I. She was confused about what she wanted to do with her life, just like me. Erin was very image conscious and so was I. She was addicted to arguing, conflict, pain, and denying the truth of her experience, just as I was. She was addicted to pretty, sex, adoration, attention, looking good, and having a good time. So was I. Erin used to lie to herself and everyone else because she believed that by herself she was not enough to be loved as a human being. She was always telling others what she thought they wanted to hear so they would accept her. I lied too, everytime I told myself that this girl loved me more than the false sense of security she derived from my money and possessions.

Saving Yourself

Trying to rescue or save others through manipulation or control is an illusion. Save yourself. Use the relationships in your life as the mirrors that they are. What you are seeing in others is a part of you; both the faults and the magnificence. Rescue yourself! Embrace the truth that your Universe is sharing with you and get about the work that is necessary in your life. Be honest. Because of my experience I now believe that many times, if not always, using the line, "I just don't know what I want," is really nothing more than a cop out. It's simply another excuse we use for not accepting responsibility for our own lives. Deep down we all know what we would really like to be doing with our lives. But if we were to acknowledge that, it would mean that we would no longer have any good reasons not to do the necessary work and become all that we could become. By seeing only the faults in others all you are doing is refusing to acknowledge the same faults in you. As you transform yourself inwardly and become committed to making your life work, your outer world will magically transform. Trust in the process. Life is the perfect process, the perfect training, for your growth into Higher Consciousness. Embrace the process. Stop resisting what Love is sharing with you. Become all that you were meant to become. Own your power and understand that you are the creator of your reality. Begin to create a reality of Love, Truth, Beauty, Peace, and Harmony.

As I look out my window and see the beautiful palm trees and the bright blue sky, as I feel the warmth of the sun and embrace the sounds and smells of the ocean, I know that it is all a mirror of my own inner beauty and tranquility. As I embrace my experience, I know that it is perfect for my growth.

OUR NEGATIVE EGO

God is always with me.

I am lifted by my Spirit.

My consciousness is transcendent.

I am forever guided by

my Higher Self.

I trust myself.

Gandhi once stated that, "The only devils in this world are the little ones running around in our own hearts and minds." Those little devils are what I call our negative ego.

We developed our negative ego as children when we began to form beliefs about our reality, about our universe, that simply were not accurate maps of the territory or the way things actually work. Our negative ego was developed out of fear. Therefore, anything we receive as direction from our negative ego is fearful and a lie. It is not the Truth, although part truths can be mixed in with the lies; which can make life very confusing. And our negative ego believes that if it were to acknowledge the existence of our Higher Self, it would cease to exist. It is therefore doing everything in its power to destroy you, for it sees you as the enemy.

Our ego was originally meant to be an assistant or messenger to convey or carry the messages and input received by our five senses to our mind. Our Mind was then supposed to evaluate this information and give it form and meaning, thereby facilitating our growth and understanding on this material plane. The problem started when we made this lowly messenger, our ego, "Chairman of the Board." We have placed it in a position of responsibility which it is simply not capable of performing. Yet it tries its best to do the job we have asked it to perform. But in the process it has become a tyrant, a monster of our own making. The reason this has happened is that we are just too lazy to think for ourselves. And in our laziness we have turned the job of thinking over to our negative ego hoping it will do the thinking for us. <u>But it cannot think</u>. That is not its function. It is a messenger in a warehouse of beliefs. All it can do is run its old programming. It's a delivery boy trying to be the Chief Executive Officer. And because it is incapable of performing the job we have given it, it tells lies to hide its incompetency.

The best way I can describe how our negative ego speaks to us is by comparing it to an evening I once spent in a tavern with some drunken friends playing liar's poker. Simply put, liar's poker is a game played with dollar bills. The serial numbers on the combined bills of all the players are used to develop your hand. But you can't see their bills and they can't see yours. So there is a lot of guessing going on. If you are caught lying you pay the other players. If they think you are lying and you're not, they pay you. (If you have never played and would like a more detailed explanation of the game go to the nearest bar and ask the bartender. I'm sure he'd be happy to show you.) My friends and I were drunk and having a great time. They were trying to make me think that what they were telling me was the truth. Each of them was trying to come up with a bigger and better lie. I was attempting to decide which of their statements were lies and which ones were the truth. That's the point of liar's poker. And when a group of liars are trying to out-lie one another, some pretty ridiculous stories can be created. Our negative ego works in much the same way.

Isolating the Voices

In her book <u>Living in the Light</u> Shakti Gawain discusses brilliantly four voices our negative ego uses to speak to many of us in an attempt to control, manipulate, and make sense of our outer reality. These four voices have been a part of my negative ego for years. By listening to these voices and believing them, I got to blame the problems in my life on others. As long as someone else was the cause of my problems I didn't have to look at the results in my life or take responsibility for making my life work. My problems were somebody else's fault. So by trying to solve everyone else's problems I didn't have to work on me. And I got to be right about my beliefs that everyone else had problems. But my life didn't work very well.

The four voices Shakti describes are <u>tyrant,</u> <u>rebel,</u> <u>victim</u> and <u>rescuer.</u> She states:

> *The tyrant and the rebel are two parts of the personality I've identified in many people I work with. The tyrant is the inner voice that tells us what we should and shouldn't do. It's all our rules and rigid expectations. It is a controlling and demanding voice. The rebel is the part of us that refuses to do anything it's told to do. It reacts in total rebellion to any controlling influence and trusts no one. When the tyrant says, 'You will do this,' the rebels says, 'No way.'*

> *The rebel was developed in early childhood in response to pressures and demands from outside authorities (parents, teachers, the church, and so on)...Our inner tyrant is developed by listening to the demanding voices of those around us...about how we should and shouldn't do things.*

> *Victim consciousness is the belief that we are helpless; that the world, people, and the economy do things to us and we have no choice but to accept what is dished out to us. It's the feeling that we can be violated from the outside without our approval.*

> *As victims, people enlist rescuers to save them. Rescuers do not know how to take care of themselves, so they focus on helping others, unconsciously trying to fulfill their own needs in an*

indirect way. They need victims to care for. A rescuer believes that others are weak or powerless and need his help.

As I isolated and worked with these voices in my life I became aware that there were also other more subtle voices which my negative ego used to speak to me. The four Gawain writes about were grosser manifestations of my negative ego. They were the loud, demanding voices which I listened to when I was focused on my outer reality. As long as I was listening to these voices I didn't have to take a good look at my life, and could focus instead on the lives and problems of others.

After I learned to quiet these grosser voices by taking responsibility for my life and observing myself much more closely, I began to isolate other more subtle voices. I also believe that there is actually only one voice speaking to us as negative ego but it uses different accents or disguises to confuse us and make us think that there are many voices. These more subtle voices are what I call <u>analyzer/promoter, supporter/controller</u>.

A Dream

One night I dreamed I was in prison. The prison was an old dilapidated house in a field surrounded by a chain link fence with a gate in it. The prison was located across the street from where I had attended high school as a teenager. There were no guards or other prisoners in my dream. The door to the house was open, as was the gate in the fence. All I had to do was walk out of the house, through the gate and be free. Yet the voices of my negative ego kept insisting that I was in prison and that escape was impossible. I knew intuitively that this was my hometown and that I wasn't in prison, but the analyzer/promoter kept telling me that I was in prison in a foreign country that just looked like my hometown, so I was afraid to leave.

The analyzer analyzes everything in its perceived reality and then attemps to give meaning to its experience. But its reality is just fearful illusions it has created and believes to be reality. The promoter promotes the ideas of the analyzer in an attempt to make you believe that the analyzer is telling you the truth. But remember we are talking about negative ego. Negative ego is created out of fear, therefore, every possible scenario thought up by the analyzer and promoted by the promoter is a lie based in fear.

As my dream progressed I decided to see if I could get out of the prison. Halfway across the field the analyzer/promoter started to whisper to me saying, "You're not wearing the right clothing. You stick out like a sore thumb. The guards are going to spot you. You don't have the right image." So I went back into the house and changed clothing. At this point the supporter/controller started speaking to me. The supporter is a fearful, weak, timid voice that supports anything. It was telling me, "These guys (meaning the analyzer/promoter) are telling you the truth, and I don't think you should go out there. I'm really afraid that you could get hurt." The controller is much more forceful and dogmatic. The controller talks loudly and demands that I listen. It defiantly proclaimed that it and the other voices were right and if I didn't listen to what they had to say, I'd be sorry. The controller forcefully backs up the supporter. In my dream they kept telling me that I was really in prison and that there was no way out, so I shouldn't even try.

The dream suddenly shifted and I found myself in France, trying to get out of the country. In my dream France symboized another type of prison. I was riding an old, beat up bicycle and riding alongside of me was a beautiful female companion of approximately my age. To the left of us was a road and to the right were houses fronted by a cobblestone sidewalk. The scene was set in a rolling, hilly landscape. Rather than getting on the road I was riding on the sidewalk. My friend was riding quietly along with me on the edge of the road. Somehow I knew she could get me out of the country. I was going over steps and porches and falling into gutters and drainage canals. She was just riding down the road. After a time my companion spoke and said she was getting tired because I was making this much too difficult. She said that she was going to go into a house to rest with some friends and that I should go on. She mentioned that she would use the road to catch up with me later. I said fine, and headed back down the sidewalk, just as I had been doing, refusing to take her hint or suggestion to get on the road.

I was then suddenly back in my hometown in this small house, or prison, listening to the supporter/controller. When they quit speaking to me, I decided once again to escape. This time I walked out to the fence, and started through the gate when the analyzer/promoter told me that they knew this looked like my hometown, but it really wasn't. They told me that I was in a foreign country without a passport and even if I got out of the prison I couldn't get across the border because the guards would spot me and shoot me. At that point the supporter/controller began speaking, trying to reinforce this belief. I then turned around, went back to the house, and the dream ended.

When I awoke the meaning was so obvious that I began to laugh. <u>The female companion was my intuition who was lovingly and gently attempting to guide and assist me</u>. I was simply refusing to follow her suggestions. All I had to do was get on the road and peddle my bicycle to get out of the country or prison, but I wanted to make it difficult and do it my way. I wanted to stay on the sidewalk more than I wanted to get out of the country, just as I wanted to stay in my little house, my box, my prison, more than I wanted to get out, because it had become so familiar to me. I then realized how much of the time I lived my life in the very same way.

Quieting the Voices

Listening to the voices of my negative ego rather than asking for and following the guidance of my Higher Self has had devastating effects in my life. If you identify with any of these voices, don't make the mistake I did for years and hate yourself for having them as part of your personality. And don't fight or argue with them. If you do, they will only scream more loudly in an attempt to be right and win the argument. What you resist, persists. Don't hate yourself or the voices. Love yourself and love the voices of your negative ego. Love the images and illusions they create. There is nothing wrong with them. They just aren't real and don't work. Embrace them, love them and as you do they will begin to be transformed. See them as the fearful little children they are, screaming for attention. Love them, listen to them, but don't believe them. Then as any child throwing a temper tantrum, once they receive the love or attention they are seeking, they will calm down and go quietly on their way. And understand that these voices are immensely powerful. As long as they remain negative nothing but chaos will be created. They will never back down in an argument. But once they see that you are not going to fight with them, you can learn to deal with them in appropriate ways. They can then have a dramatic positive impact in your life. They can be transformed into a positive ego.

It is also very easy to recognize when these voices are speaking to you. Your emotions will tell you. When these voices are speaking your emotional world will be one of uneasiness. You will feel afraid and uncomfortable. These voices will always start clamoring for attention whenever some part of their illusory world seems threatened. They are voices of your addictive, inaccurate belief system. They are concerned only with attack and vengeance. The gifts they offer are pain and condemnation. Your Higher Self offers only love and forgiveness. So any time you feel uneasy, jealous, fearful, angry, or emotionally upset in any way, one or more of these voices is speaking to you, and they are speaking to you from a faulty belief which you hold and are addicted to.

Becoming conscious of these voices in your life can be one of the most productive things you can ever do. As you begin to isolate and understand these voices you will learn to differentiate between the voices of your negative ego and the lies they tell and the voice and direction of your intuition, your Higher Self. Ask your Higher Self for help in working with your negative ego, and do what it instructs you to do. As you learn to follow the direction of your Higher Self, your feminine intuitive energy, your intention will become much clearer and what you truly desire will begin to manifest itself in your reality. At times it can happen so quickly that it will absolutely amaze you.

Acknowledge your power to create the life you desire. You can have it all. Acknowledge your own perfection. And see that perfection doesn't mean that you know and understand everything there is to know in the Universe or that you will never again make a miscalculation. But it does mean that your body--the instrument of perception through which you have chosen to experience life at this time (which is a combination of both spiritual matter, your Higher Self, and physical matter, your body with its marvelous physical senses) is perfect. You have everything you need to learn and grow. Love yourself just as you are. Love yourself as an ever unfolding process. There will always be more to learn and comprehend, on this and other planes of existence. Perfection is not a static state. We will never stop progressing. Life is eternal. Life is a process of learning to do what works. You too are eternal. Your Higher Self and Love know that. They are simply waiting lovingly for the child within you—your negative ego still trusting in its fear—to realize this and to acknowledge the Truth. And Love will wait, for as long as it takes, for each of us to grow up.

CREATING INTIMACY
WITH YOURSELF

To know myself is to love myself.
I am intimate with myself
in all ways.
I seek only the truth.
I am worthy.
I surrender to God.

Let me share an exercise I have found to be very useful to me. First isolate the voices you identify with as part of your ego self, and write them down on a piece of paper: Tyrant, rebel, victim, rescuer, analyzer, promoter, supporter, controller. Perhaps you have other voices. Whatever they are, write them down.

Next, go to a quiet place where you will be undisturbed and sit down in a comfortable position. Then close your eyes and visualize your Higher Self as a compassionate, loving, caring, gentle, all-knowing woman. She can be your spouse, a dear friend, a mother figure, or simply a beautiful creation of your ideal female. Then in your mind's eye notice all of the different voices of your negative ego gathered around you and see that they are children. Your Higher Self is in the center, like the hub of a wheel and the children are circled around You. They are facing away from the center. Their energies are being directed outwardly. Notice how each is dressed. The rebel in me is a young boy of eleven or twelve years of age with long, straggly hair, wearing blue jeans and a leather biking jacket, smoking a cigarette. He is telling the whole world to get screwed. The promoter is a young man who wears eight hundred dollar suits and always has new ideas and better ways to do things. Let these voices be what they are for you. As your Higher Self sits in the midst of these young children of your ego self, a conversation ensues. Visualize this loving maternal self asking questions of the children and then listen to what they are saying to you. Talk with them and become familiar with each of their voices. Ask them why they do what they do. Perhaps you can ask the controller why he is always trying to control the situations outside of himself, or why he is so afraid. Or ask the supporter why he feels so afraid and victimized. Ask whatever it is you want to ask them. Listen to what they have to say and love them just as they are. Then tell them how much you love them and begin to teach them new ways to view life and themselves. Teach your controller that the most effective way to expend his energy is by learning to control himself and that you love him just as he is. Share with the rescuer that his energies could best be spent by rescuing himself. Slowly you notice that they are turning towards your Higher Self. One by one, they turn inwardly toward the center. Perhaps they come you and you embrace them and share your love with them. Perhaps you cry with them, and they with you. Listen to their pain and their reasons for acting the way they do. Listen to their fears. Then begin to teach them appropriate ways to channel their energies and share with them that by working together a new and better life can be created for all.

I have learned to let this meditation go wherever it takes me, and I just keep finding new ways of expressing love. Sometimes I have envisioned my female intuitive self begin to spin counter-clockwise and turn into a brilliant cylinder of Light and Love which engulfs the children and transforms them. As each child surrenders and steps into the Light, they are consumed by the fire of the Light and we become as one. It is as though they are sacrificing themselves one by one for the Higher Good of the Whole. And the Light grows ever brighter. After this merging of the children and mother, my male aspect comes onto the scene and together the female and male join in sexual union and a new Child is born. This Child is a Being of great Love and Compassion. It is a Child of Light, and the Love that both parents feel for this Child and for one another is incomprehensible. The Love this Child expresses towards the parents is equal in magnitude and as the Child grows and expands the parents are consumed in the fire of His Love. Together they become One. And the Higher Self is born into complete conscious awareness to take his rightful place as the Orchestrator of His True Destiny.

This exercise has helped me develop more intimacy with myself than any other meditation I have ever done. As I have learned to love each of the different aspects of my ego and to become more intimate with my ego, my sensitivity and ability to be intimate with myself and with others in the world has increased dramatically. As each child of my negative ego has experienced more love over time, the love and the trust between my Higher Self and my negative ego has increased. And my negative ego has been transformed into a positive ego and has become a more integrated helpful part of my personality.

Other times I envision both my female and male counterparts teaching together as loving parents. The voices of my ego are their children and together they learn and grow as a family. The controller learns to listen and quietly control his inner world. The analyzer learns to relax rather than expending its energy ineffectively by analyzing the events and people in my outer world. The promoter learns to promote ideas of my Higher Self which will create a better life for me. The supporter learns to support my Higher Self and the Truth she shares. And so on.

By learning to integrate your ego and your Higher Self and allowing them to work together in appropriate, healthy ways, a new life of Love and fulfillment can be yours. This meditation is powerful, if practiced with Love.

LISTENING TO LOVE

God is Love.

I am Love.

I always listen.

I hear the voice of God.

I am aware that I am unaware.

The answers are within.

I have talked in various chapters about the ways in which Love speaks to us, but I would like to share in more detail a few daily practices that can increase your sense of purpose and direct your life in more appropriate ways.

Listening is a skill I have had to work on my entire life. In my relationships and business dealings my failure to listen and understand the other side's point of view has caused more problems than any other single factor I can think of, except failing to listen to my intuition.

Love, or your Higher Self, is always willing to guide you if you will learn to listen and follow its direction. But to hear the voice of your Higher Self you must learn to quiet your mind. I have found that one of the most essential things I can do to stay in touch with my Higher Self is to take ten or fifteen minutes each morning and afternoon or evening to be alone by myself and relax. Relax my body, emotions and thoughts, and listen. If you practice a form of meditation, it will work just fine. If you feel more comfortable praying, that is all right. What is important is to relax at least twice a day and to be by yourself for a few minutes. If you have never done this before, don't make it into something difficult, mysterious or religious. It is simply fifteen minutes of relaxation. A time to collect your thoughts and feelings by letting them all go.

Learning to Quiet Your Noisy Mind

Let me share with you what I do. At the age of 18 I was introduced to Transcendental Meditation. A mantra, or sound, is used in TM that allows your mind to focus on just one thing. If you would like to do this, try it. Perhaps you could use the word <u>Emma</u>. This is a feminine given name meaning whole or universal.

Sit in a relaxed, comfortable position, perhaps in your favorite chair or sofa and close your eyes. Now simply repeat the word Emma silently to yourself. Sometimes you may want to repeat it quickly. Other times it may feel more comfortable to repeat it slowly. As other thoughts come to mind don't wrestle with them, but just allow them to float by. When you become aware that you are no longer repeating the word Emma, begin to repeat it again, silently to yourself. Do this for about fifteen minutes each morning and evening. I have found it to be very relaxing and a wonderful way to release tension.

Another form of relaxation that I enjoy is to put on some very soothing music. I like Pachebel's Canon in D, but anything you find that relaxes you will do. Next, sit in a comfortable position and close your eyes. As the music plays, notice your feet and ankles. Move them around. Flex the muscles in your feet and ankles, then release the tension. Feel a deep, warm sense of relaxation come into them. Then move up your body and do the same with your calf muscles. Tense the muscles, then release. Become relaxed. Next your thighs, then your buttocks and hips. Move up your back and to your neck. Rotate your head in a circular motion to stretch and relax the muscles. Then tense and relax your eye and facial muscles, your jaws, your shoulders, your arms and hands. And finally, relax your chest and stomach muscles. You are then completely relaxed. Next imagine a beautiful white light which begins to grow and magnify at the base of your spine. It slowly moves up your spinal column into your neck and head, and flows over into your eyes and face, and down through each cell of your body, through each organ, and finally into your feet. As this light pulsates within you in rhythm to your breathing or heartbeat, imagine it is cleansing every cell of your body and healing your body with its love and light. And sometimes other things happen. Just go wherever the meditation takes you, and enjoy it.

Guides

There is one other exercise I sometimes perform which oftentimes takes me to wonderful places. Use the music and relax the different muscle groups as before. Then picture yourself in a beautiful forest. See yourself walking down a path in the forest. As you walk deeper and deeper into the forest you see the trees, the plants, the beautiful sunlight, and the morning dew on the leaves. Everything is peaceful and safe. You are a part of this beautiful forest. As you follow this path, ever deeper into the forest, up ahead you see someone walking toward you. Perhaps you know this person, or maybe you have never met. As you come closer, you notice a beautiful light surrounding them and you feel a deep warmth and attraction for them. As you meet, you embrace and greet one another. This person then begins to speak to you. This friend shares with you something that only you could know. You then ask this wonderful being of Light questions. Questions about anything, your relationships, your career, your life purpose, your feelings, your emotions, whatever. Then you listen. Listen to what this wise, loving teacher has to share with you. The results of listening to this loving person can be miraculous.

After you have asked your questions and listened to this kind, warm, caring companion, you say goodbye, knowing that you can return to this place whenever you like and learn from your counselor and guide. After you have said goodby, when you are ready, slowly open your eyes.

When you perform these exercises, remember the most important thing is to relax. Be sensitive and flow with the experience. This way each experience can be different and show you different aspects of yourself: your thoughts, fears, tensions, anxieties, and emotions. It is a wonderful way to begin your day and to release any tensions in the afternoon or evening.

Listening is wonderful. Listening is relaxing. Listen to your body, to its gentle loving vibrations during these meditations. And just allow any other thoughts to flow through your mind. This is your way of letting go and releasing things in your life which you have been holding on to. Release them and any tension you may have associated with them. Release your guilt and your anxiety. And as you do feel the Love of the Universe take their place. Let these moments be another way in which you are sharing Love with yourself.

Listening Works

By learning to quiet your thoughts whenever life becomes confusing and to drop into a deeper place within to ask for guidance from your Higher Self, your life can change dramatically. For example, let's say your spouse and you are having a disagreement. You are beginning to feel uneasy and upset. This should indicate two things to you. First, that you are reacting from an addictive behavior pattern. And second, one or more of the voices used by your negative ego is speaking to you, causing the discomfort and creating unnecessary stress in your relationship. At this point you should acknowledge your addiction. In most cases it will be an addiction about being right, which of course places your spouse erroneously in a position of being wrong. Close your eyes for a moment and go to this deeper place within. Ask your Higher Self what should be done in the situation so that the Love between you and your spouse might grow, rather than diminish. Then listen! You might hear a small voice from within telling you to listen to his/her side and surrender your position. You might simply have a feeling about the situation. You may feel an urge to put your arms around him/her and apologize. Or you may feel a need to excuse yourself for a moment so you can have more time to quiet your thoughts and emotions. <u>Your ability to love is proportionate to your ability to understand that which you are trying to love</u>. Is the topic you are disagreeing on really serious enough to become angry over? Will your anger towards one another solve the problem or intensify it? As you learn to listen to and trust your intuition, you will find miracles can occur in your relationships.

When I am making a financial or business decision I have found listening to my intuition can be very helpful. Almost every time I have made a financial decision that hasn't worked out as well as I would have liked, the decision was made without giving myself time to search my feelings and consult my intuition. If you are having difficulty discerning which voice is your voice, the voice of your Higher Self, learn to pay more attention to your emotions. The voice of your Higher Self will feel strong, yet gentle. It feels direct, supporting, calm, confident and comforting. The voices of your negative ego do not feel comforting. They feel and sound excited. They are always impatient, in a hurry and anxious. When they are speaking you will feel confused, unsure, fearful or <u>sensually over excited and stimulated</u>. This uneasiness should indicate to you that this is not your Higher Self speaking to you.

Learning to listen more effectively to others and yourself can change your life. By listening, the solutions to your problems can be found. By listening you will discover that <u>there are no problems in life, but rather a resistance to seeking the solutions to what we call problems</u>. Listening does not mean that we are thinking about what we are going to say the next time we have the opportunity to speak. <u>Effective listening is the first step towards understanding, which in a very real sense is Loving</u>.

As you learn to listen you will begin to notice much less tension in your life. As you learn to listen you will notice that your mind and the voices of your negative ego will become much less noisy and not nearly so demanding of your constant attention. And in this calm, peaceful silence you will begin to recognize, hear, and understand the Voice of Love more easily in your daily life. You will also find that the voice of your Higher Self does have the answers to your questions.

Practice and More Practice

In your morning and afternoon relaxation periods ask the Love within you questions about anything that seems important to you, and learn to listen to the answers. Perhaps you would like a better relationship with your children or spouse. Ask Love, or your Higher Self, what you could personally do to improve these relationships. Then listen and act on what you receive. Maybe you want to know what you could do to improve your financial position in life. Ask for guidance. Love will give it to you. Or perhaps you would like to know how you could find more fulfillment in your career. Ask! Answers will come.

Be open to possibilities. Two years ago I would never have considered writing a book. I didn't like writing letters, let alone a book. Yet as I began asking for direction in my life and career, I kept getting the same answer, "Write a book!" So I did, and writing has become one of the greatest joys of my life. It has enhanced my financial situation and opened up many new doors of opportunity which I had never dreamed of before. And it all came about because I finally learned to ask for direction and to listen to what came to me.

I have also learned to listen in other ways. Many times I have asked for help and I haven't heard or felt anything. But I have learned to be patient and continue to ask for guidance in my heart and mind, either through meditation, prayer, or both. Invariably, something eventually happens. A friend might call and through our conversation I receive my answer. Or someone will tell me to read a certain book or attend a seminar and, bingo, I find my answers. They always come if I am patient and paying attention to my Universe. Love's patience is unending and I have found that Love's timetable does not always coincide with mine, especially when I am working from an addiction which says, "I want it, and I want it right now." But I have learned that Love or my Higher Self, knows all things. Love has always revealed Its reasons for making me wait. I have learned to be grateful for this. And through the waiting I have learned a very profound lesson about life. <u>Anything worth having takes patience and effort. If it didn't, you wouldn't appreciate or value it once you attained it</u>.

Learning to listen with a loving heart and waiting on Love's guidance and direction is well worth the effort one must put forth and the patience one must exercise. Miracles do happen!

DEVELOPING SENSITIVITY

I am powerful.

I own my power.

I use my power to bless others.

Love is the greatest power.

I allow others to experience their

experience.

Have you ever walked into a room where two or more people have just had a bitter argument? The screaming and anger have subsided, but as you entered what did you feel? What was your experience? You probably noticed the cold, gray silence that exists after such arguments. And the feeling was as real as anything you have ever felt. You knew an argument had just taken place. The emptiness you felt was the absence of Love.

How many times have you been thinking of a certain song or thought and someone around you starts singing the very same melody or speaking the same thought? Remember how amazed you were? We say things like, "My, isn't that a coincidence? I was just thinking the same thing." There is nothing coincidental about it. It is simply a matter of subtle physics.

When someone close to you begins to speak what you have just been thinking, understand what is taking place. Our auras, or the fields of energy which our Spirits create extend much further out from us than we realize. When a thought occurs, an electrical impulse is created. It originates in our mind, and if it is our intention for this thought to move our hand to pick up an object, or to get a drink of water, or to speak, the impulse is directed through the neurons of our brain to the appropriate parts of our body so the task can be completed. It is electricity, and when the thought, the electrical spark occurs, it also goes outward in all directions. And just as a pebble dropping into a pool of water creates a wave formation, our thoughts create waves or vibrations in our energy fields, our auras, which can be picked up by others in a conscious manner, if they are sensitive enough and open enough to be receptive. They then begin to sing the song or speak the thought. We call that coincidence.

An example of this was reported by scientists in 1952. It is called the Hundredth-Monkey Syndrome. In Japan scientists were studying the behavior of wild monkeys. The main foodstuff of the monkeys was sweet potatoes. One day one of the monkeys washed a potato before eating it. This was something the scientists had never observed before. Soon all of the monkeys on that island were washing their potatoes. Then in 1958 scientists on other islands began reporting that monkeys there also had begun to wash their sweet potatoes before eating them. No monkeys from the island where this phenomenon had first been reported had been transferred to any of the other islands or had any type of physical interaction with monkeys from other islands.

This study demonstrates the power that our thoughts can and do have. Learning to become more sensitive to your thoughts and feelings, as well as the thoughts and feelings of others, can create wonderful opportunities. Your thoughts give life to all of creation. Your power is much greater than you have ever imagined. Do not be afraid because you do not fully understand how to control or direct your thoughts at this point in time. Blocking the Love by becoming fearful will only hinder your growth and development. You simply begin by listening to the thoughts Love is sharing with you through your Higher Self, your intuition. In time Love's thoughts will become your thoughts. It's that simple, although it seems very complex. <u>All that is complex can be made simple, and all that is simple can be made complex</u>. Through prayer, meditation and asking for Love to guide you, and by listening, you will be able to develop these abilities to a much greater extent. "Knock and it shall be opened unto you. Ask and ye shall receive." Enjoy your power. Learn to play with your power in appropriate ways as directed by Love. Practice with your telepathic abilities. You already use them to a much greater extent than you realize. Become conscious of your powers. Send mental messages to your friends and loved ones and watch what happens. As you become more conscious over time, you will discover more power and ability. Learn to quiet your thoughts and emotions through relaxation so you can become more sensitive to the enormity of your whole being. As you do, miracles will happen in your life and in the lives of those around you.

FREEDOM

I am free to choose.

I allow others their freedom.

I seek my Highest Good.

I emulate the Highest.

Life is an opportunity not an

obligation.

What does individual freedom mean to you? Love has shown me that freedom, like everything else, is a paradox. It is a sword that cuts both ways.

I remember taking piano lessons as a child. I practiced for awhile and learned to play a few songs that I really didn't enjoy and finally became bored with the whole process. I told myself that practicing the piano hindered my freedom; the freedom to go out and play with my friends or watch TV. And the truth was that it did. Soon I began to place more importance on playing with my friends or whatever else it was I wanted to do at the time, than practicing and learning to play the piano. What I got to have was the temporary freedom of the moment. But by not being clear about my long-term intention, the freedom I don't have now is the freedom to sit down at a piano and play anything I want to play. The long-term, enduring freedom to create music on the piano that only comes with self discipline, dedication, and commitment is not mine to enjoy. And so it is with all other aspects of life.

Choices

Your life and mine is an endless matter of choice. We have the freedom to choose daily between mediocrity or greatness, abundance or scarcity, pleasure or pain, fear or Love. The choice is ours. We each have been endowed with gifts and talents. We have the freedom to develop these talents and enjoy a greater freedom which comes only by accepting the responsibility of manifesting and becoming all that we are capable of becoming. We can choose to see ourselves as creators of a meaningful, beautiful life. Or we can choose to ignore the gifts and talents we were born with and live a much lesser form of existence. We are free to choose to hold onto the beliefs and reasons we use to rationalize and justify our perhaps less than abundant and fulfilled lives. We have the freedom to see ourselves as victims of circumstance, unable to grow or change. And we have the freedom to confuse laziness and rebellion with freedom, as I have done many times in my life by running from my responsibility to myself.

<u>Life, the reality you create, is nothing more and nothing less than what you believe it to be.</u> Your manifest, physical reality is created by your beliefs and assumptions. You can choose to deny that. You do have that freedom, but it will never change the fact that it is the truth. And such denial will never bring about the results you desire.

True freedom, the greater freedom which Love offers you each moment, is the freedom to choose to be all that you can be, all that you already are, and through commitment to that truth create the manifest reality your Higher Self would have you create. You are free to choose either abundance or scarcity in all aspects of your life. And commitment to becoming all that you can become is the only thing that will bring about the fulfillment and joy, the life and Love, that you are seeking.

What Love, or God, your Higher Self, is actually doing is incarnating on this material plane of existence through us. Love, God, Goddess, All That Is, wants to share and spread Its Love throughout the Universe. It wants to bring the Love we all enjoyed in our Spiritual existence, before our lives began on this material plane here to this place in time. It wants to bring heaven to earth. And Love needs you to do it, because you are an integral part of Love.

Most of us have lived our lives in fear, and what have the results been? Isn't it true that we have all experienced and shared far more pain and suffering than we would like to admit? Isn't it true that we would really like more happiness and Love in each of our lives? And we can have it. So much of the time we choose in desperation to try to rearrange the people or things in our lives to fit into our expectations of what life should be. We think that if we can rearrange our outer world, that somehow we will change our inner world, our world of thoughts and emotions. But it doesn't work that way. <u>Your outer reality can never change your mind or your beliefs, but your mind and beliefs can be changed</u>. They can be released. You have that power. You possess that freedom. And when you change your mind, your world view, your belief systems, miracles will occur.

The outer, manifest reality you have created is nothing more or less than a reflection of your inner reality. Your reality of beliefs. "If ye have faith, as a grain of mustard seed, ye shall say unto this mountain, 'Remove hence to yonder place'; and it shall remove; and nothing shall be impossible unto you."

Doing What Works

Come to truly know yourself by observing yourself. And by observing yourself, you will begin to understand how you work as a human being, and how you use beliefs and programming to create your reality. By changing your beliefs and assumptions, the way you view the world, you can literally transform your reality. The problem is that most of us have it backwards. We are trying to physically manipulate, control and rearrange our outer reality in an attempt to influence and make a difference inwardly. That is simply not how it works. Change the inner you, change your beliefs so that they are accurate maps of the territory, and you will find what you have always been looking for in your outer reality. The choice is your's to make. You are free to choose between what works and what doesn't work.

I've learned, and many times the hard way because I chose to make it hard, that the greater freedoms in life come only through dedication, work and commitment to doing what works. Many times I have made my life very difficult because I have been so addicted to doing things that didn't work. Changing course can be scary, but in the end, it is the only way. Why are we so afraid of making our lives work? Why are we afraid of doing what works? <u>Fear always indicates addiction</u>. We are afraid to let go of what we know, what has become familiar to us.

My relationships were frequently difficult because my maps weren't accurately describing my present situation. They were maps and beliefs depicting my childhood, my past experience or an illusion my negative ego had created. So when the relationships got rocky, I tried to rearrange my outer world by attempting to change or rescue the other person rather than getting clear about my intention and what I truly wanted from a relationship. I exercised my freedom to do that. I kept choosing the same types of partners because I was unconscious of my intention. And the greater freedom, the freedom that comes from relationships of commitment, to doing what works, was never mine. Only after two people have practiced the art of loving in relationship to one another and have developed appropriate beliefs that work, will they ever know the greater freedom. The freedom to live and grow together in a celebration of life. To share the beautiful music of their Love together. And to create a reality of Love, a home filled with Love, where their children can dance and play to the music their Love has created. <u>And it is commitment that makes the difference</u>.

Prices and Consequences

The same freedom can manifest itself in your careers. Your career, the way you make your living, could be an expression of you, of your gifts and talents as a child of Love. All of us have gifts, talents to be nurtured, and by developing them our line of work could become a form of play that we get paid for. I love writing and teaching. And people pay me to do it. I have friends who love to develop real estate. It is a talent they have. They make their living by expressing who they are. I have friends who are musicians, and they love their work. And it is much easier to be committed to something you love, than to something you despise or fear. The choice is yours. You are free to choose every moment of your life. <u>But you are not free from the consequences of your choices, and you never will be</u>. Your life is your responsibility. I know that at times it can appear easier to run from the responsibilities of becoming all that we can become rather than developing our gifts and talents. The immediate sensual freedom of laziness is so enticing. But responsibility cuts both ways. Having to take responsibility for the consequences of a non-productive, wasted life of mediocrity lived on a completely sensual level is devastating. It is a very heavy price to pay. Love has shown me that the lesser freedoms are illusions. It is not freedom at all to run from the responsibility we each have to develop our gifts and talents, the responsibility to become all that we can become, all that we were created to become. <u>To run from that, in an attempt to exercise our freedom, our free will, is to run as fast as we can to a self-made prison full of the pain and suffering that are the results of unrealized dreams and aspirations</u>. But Love loves us enough to allow us that freedom. If we don't want the guidance Love would offer us, Love will not force it upon us. Love wants us to learn what really works. "Seek and you shall find; ask and it shall be given unto you." All things are possible with Love. And Love's greatest freedoms can be yours if you so desire. The choice is yours.

The Paradox of Sin

<u>To sin is to do that which doesn't work</u>, that which keeps you from reaching your highest potential. To sin is to go against the direction of your Higher Self, or Love. To sin is to not be all of who you already are. <u>And sin is not an act that requires punishment or penance, but rather a mistaken choice which needs correction</u>. Every moment you have a chance to choose differently. But to choose to live by the direction and guidance of your Higher Self, you must engage in the inner dialogue between Love, your Higher Self, and your ego or mind. If you choose to sin, that doesn't mean you are bad, that you are sinful by nature, or that Love will cease loving you, but your life won't work. And your power will diminish. Sin weakens us. Each time we sin we lose self respect and confidence in ourselves. To sin is to not love yourself. Love, God, Goddess, All That Is, will still love you and want the best for you. Love does not reject or condemn you because you are still growing. So don't reject yourself. Forgive yourself. Forgiving is letting go of and releasing the past. The past is an illusion. It's gone and there is nothing you can do about it. Yet the paradox lies in the fact that what we forget or become unconscious of we will repeat.

And isn't it true that every time you have made a decision or choice, that at the time you thought you were making the best choice possible? You thought in the moment that you were choosing what was in your own best interest. So why beat yourself up for doing the best you could do at the time. And realizing this, do you see the paradox? **There is no sin!** Living life consciously is a fine line to walk. But living consciously is the only way we can succeed. Love yourself and be all that you can be, all that you were meant to be. Create the life you desire. Then live in the joy and happiness of your creation.

EXPRESSING LOVE
FOR YOURSELF

I observe my words.

I know my words reflect my beliefs.

I learn quickly.

I am a process.

I embrace change.

I am perfect in the eye's of God.

How much do you really love yourself? Have you ever thought seriously about this question? How often and in what ways do you express love for yourself? How do you talk to yourself about yourself? The voices we use when we talk to ourselves are what I call Self-Talk. Sometimes we talk out loud, but often we speak silently to ourselves about ourselves. When I began learning about Love, I became conscious of how I spoke to myself; what my Self-Talk was about. And quite honestly, I was shocked. I found that in many ways I despised myself.

For most of my adult life I had abused myself physically with drugs and alcohol. I never exercised and had no regard for what I ate or drank. Consequently, I caused a great amount of pain in my life and in the lives of those closest to me.

For ten years, almost daily, I went to bars, got drunk, used drugs, mostly cocaine, smoked cigarettes, and had endless one night stands. I'd wake up the next morning, if I'd gone to bed, feeling horrible and hating myself for having done it again. I would get up and call myself every awful name possible. I verbally beat myself silly. I told myself that I was stupid, weak, and basically just a rotten person. I'd talk to myself this way until the guilt was so great I couldn't hold any more. Then I told myself that this was absolutely the last time. I told myself I'd never drink or do drugs again, and then went about doing whatever it was I had to do that day. And I carried the guilt around with me all day long. By the time the evening rolled around and I was feeling better physically, I went back to the bars to escape from the guilt. It was a vicious circle, a nightmare with no visible means of escape. I simply thought that I wasn't strong enough or good enough to overcome these things. And no matter how hard I tried to do what didn't work, it still didn't work. No matter how guilty I made myself feel, my behavior didn't change. My wife left me, I was burning out badly at my job, and I spent a lot more money than I was making. But my habits remained unchanged. I just couldn't see a way to do things differently that worked.

The Beginning of the Process

Just before my wife left I saw the movie "Gandhi." This movie caused a major shift in my consciousness. He had become conscious about many things in his life that I just wasn't seeing in mine. So I read every book Gandhi had written or that had been written about him. Slowly I began to learn about Love. I began to learn about loving myself.

One of the first things I became aware of was my Self-Talk. I made myself sound like the worst person in the world. I didn't do this when I was talking to others about myself. I had an image to protect. But when I talked to myself about myself, it was a different story. As time went by I began to see that deep down inside I knew I wasn't as awful as I made myself sound. So I began to take inventory of my Self-Talk. I actually started writing down what I was saying to myself. I then turned it around. Rather than telling myself negative things about myself, I changed them into positive statements or affirmations. I know it sounds too simple, but it worked.

I told myself that I was a wonderful, strong, loving person, and magic began to happen in my life. As I expressed more love for myself by talking to myself in more loving ways, the desire to abuse myself with drugs and alcohol just went away. It didn't happen overnight, but the more love I expressed towards myself, the faster it happened. Looking back I see that the cocaine and alcohol were simply physical manifestations of the mental, emotional, and verbal abuse I was inflicting upon myself. I was actually programming my mind to carry out these sick, addictive patterns of behavior by talking so negatively to myself. I was the creator of my own nightmare, but too unconscious to see what I was doing. My outer reality was nothing more or less than a reflection of my inner beliefs, and mental programming. <u>I now see that all forms of physical abuse and sickness are self-inflicted and directly related to a lack of self love</u>.

So, how do you talk to you? See if any of these voices are familiar:

"I'm so unorganized."
"Why can't things ever go right."
"I never remember names."
"I just can't seem to lose weight."
"I wish I were a millionaire."
"I never have enough money."
"Why can't I ever be on time?"
"I'm not attractive."
"It's just one of those days."
"I just don't have any patience."
"Why does everyone else have all the luck?"
"I can't do that."
"I was just never any good at that."
"Nobody appreciates me."

The list goes on and on. It's endless. And the words seem like harmless little words. But they create your reality. Every time you talk to yourself this way you are programming your mind to create a similar outer reality. Do you see how powerful you are? Most of us have been talking to ourselves in such ways for years, completely unaware of it. And guess what? You have become exactly what you have been telling yourself you are. If you tell yourself you're not good at remembering names, I'll bet you're not. That doesn't mean you couldn't be good at remembering names. You simply hold a belief that says you're not and you want to be right about your belief.

Transference

Some real problems occur when our minds begin to do what psychologists call transference. Let me give you an example. Let's say that you believe that you are unlovable. This does not make you unlovable. <u>You just believe that you are</u>. So your negative ego tries to come up with a way to manifest this belief physically, and perhaps you begin to overeat. After a time you become grossly overweight. And sure enough, nobody wants to go out with you. And you get to be right about your belief. But you also have a driving need to be loved, as we all do. Your negative ego then confuses love with the sensual pleasure you derive from eating whatever it is you like to eat. Your mind transfers the need to be loved onto your addictive eating patterns and begins to believe love is pleasure. It gets so confusing you have no idea that overeating is a symptom of your belief that you are unlovable. So you can't see any solution. You go on a hundred different diets, but they never work.

For years I had love confused with sex, drugs, alcohol, cigarettes, and almost everything else. I kept chopping away at the branches, rather than the roots of my problems. And the branches kept growing back. External problems will never go away until the internal causes are resolved--until your beliefs are changed and your mind reprogrammed. It's that simple, and at the same time that complex.

So if there are things in your life that you are not happy with and would really like to change, you can. You have everything available to you to live a full, happy, productive life. <u>You are not deficient in any way</u>, except in your understanding of how you work as a human being. "Know thyself and the Truth shall make you free." All the information pertinent to a fulfilling, productive life is available to you simply for the asking. Love will share it with you, if and <u>when you are ready to hear and accept it</u>.

If you want to change any aspect of your life, acknowledge that desire. Acknowledge that it's a problem for you and acknowledge yourself for having the courage and desire to grow and become. Whether it's a drug problem, a weight problem, or any other behavioral problem, begin by loving yourself. Accept yourself just as you are and know that you are enough. Love your addictions, no matter how sick they appear to be. Love yourself just as you are. And don't be afraid. For where there is fear and guilt there is no Love. And where there is Love, there is no fear or guilt. Forgive yourself for beating yourself up for all this time. It's okay. Acknowledge the child within you who wants to learn and grow and be loved. For whosoever shall humble himself as a little child, the same is greatest in the Kingdom of Heaven. And whosoever shall receive such a child in Love's name, receiveth me, for I am Love.

Looking back I see my struggle with drugs and alcohol as great learning experiences. They were some of my best friends at that time in my life. They were killing me, but they were always there for me, and taught me a great deal about myself. As I learned new and better ways of loving myself, I found new and better friends. So can you. You can have whatever you want, once you are clear about what it is you want.

Reprogramming

Write down the ways in which you talk to yourself as I did and rephrase the sentences. It worked for me. And notice I said "work" because that's what it takes. Take each voice or sentence you use and make it into a positive one:

"I am lucky."
"I will not be abandoned in my relationships."
"I can lose weight easily."
"I am a wonderful person."
"I am lovable."
"I am successful."
"I am worthy."
"I am deserving."
"I am intelligent."
"I am a talented, gifted person."
"I am attractive."
"Anything is possible in my life."
"I learn with out resistance."
"I can do anything I set my mind to do."

As you learn to express love towards yourself, miracles will occur in your life. As you express more love for yourself, you will find yourself becoming much more sensitive to the whisperings of Love within and the direction it has to offer you. Learn to listen to its sweet, soft voice.

Another exercise I would recommend is to write a "love letter" to yourself. Imagine that you are writing to the most wonderful person in the world. You are writing a letter to your Prince/Princess Charming and your heart, mind, body, and soul are filled with love and ecstasy for this person. Express your deepest desires, hopes, and dreams in this letter. Share your most intimate feelings and thoughts. But write it to yourself! Let the Love in your heart overflow and fill the pages of this letter with your greatest aspirations. Be gentle, caring, giving, and kind in the letter. And know that you are the person for whom this love was meant. Shower yourself with love. Then mail it to yourself. Read it and cherish each word and sentiment. This can be a powerful, transformational experience. The next time life seems to be swallowing you up, read the letter again. Over time, if you would like to add to this letter, do so. You could write many such letters to yourself. And as you do, know that you are every bit as wonderful as the letter says. Love yourself just as you are!

ACCOUNTABILITY AND INTENTION

I am the creator of my reality.

I am accountable for my life.

My results prove my intention.

What I have is what I want.

I can have anything I want.

I am clear about what I want.

We must assume accountability for our own lives if we are ever going to achieve true fulfillment. We are each accountable for our lives and present situations. Until you accept this principle as reality, what you are saying in effect is, "I am not responsible or accountable for my life. I am a victim of circumstance and powerless to change my life. It's just not my fault." Well, you can live your life from that point of view, but has it worked so far?

Webster defines accountability as, "personal responsibility, the ability to act without guidance or superior authority; being the source or cause of something." So what is it for which you are accountable? To what are you committed?

Are you accountable for your thoughts and feelings, or do other people and events cause them? If your relationships aren't working, who's accountable? Perhaps you own a business and your company is having difficulty. Who's accountable? Or maybe you plan an outing with your family and it rains all weekend. Who's accountable for that? Do you think or believe that things just happen to you? Do people and outside circumstances victimize you? Do you believe there are accidents? Is your life working sometimes or all the time? Are you accountable for everything that happens to you, or just some things?

If you are having difficulty answering these questions, you're not alone. There is a tremendous payoff for being a victim. You get to believe in accidents. It doesn't have to be your fault and you can blame someone or something else when things go badly.

If something unexpected happens, you look to see who is at fault. Once you've identified who's at fault, you know who to blame. Then you understand what happened. And you get to be right about your understanding. The problem is that understanding doesn't change anything. Knowing who's at fault and who to blame doesn't do anything about the problem. Nothing ever gets solved by fixing blame and finding fault. If there is no one to blame for the problem, you call the unexpected result an accident and write it off to fate. You experience yourself as a victim.

Accountability has nothing to do with fixing blame, finding fault and having accidents. Blaming yourself for what happens and finding fault in yourself only produces guilt. Like fear, guilt is produced by withholding love from yourself. Accountability is not motivated by the need to control people and circumstances. It is the realization that you create your own life. You are powerful enough to actualize the results in your life. You are the cause in your life. Your intention produces your results. You are accountable for everything. That may seem like an overwhelming responsibility. But there are no limits to your power. The more accountability you assume, the more conscious you become, and the more powerful you become. There is no need to blame others or to be a victim of circumstances. Blaming, fault-finding, guilt, and victimization are ways you give your power away by denying accountability.

Have you ever considered the possibility that you are accountable for <u>everything</u>? And how large a category is <u>everything</u>? Everything in your immediate living context? Everything in your family? Everything in your neighborhood, your city, your county, your state, your country, your planet, your universe? You are the source of your experience of everything. That may be a sobering thought. It may sound crazy. How could you, just you, be accountable for all the poverty, violence, pain, and suffering in your life and in this world? And how could you be accountable for all the greatness, compassion, spirituality, and genius in your life and in this world? Accountability works both ways. Is that proposition absolutely unthinkable to you? Seeing the boundaries of personal accountability and integrity in such all encompassing terms is a profound realization. And it might seem easier, in the short run, not to be accountable and to blame others for everything unpleasant that happens. But has it been working for you?

Two Propositions

Look at your life. What do you have? What don't you have? What do you want? What don't you want? What are the results of having lived your life to this point? This chapter works from two related propositions. The extent to which you find yourself resisting these propositions is the extent to which there is room for you to learn and to discover dimensions of power and accountability in your life. The first proposition is: <u>What you have is what you want</u>. The second proposition is: <u>What you want is what you have</u>. The implication of these two propositions is that you are accountable for what you've created. <u>What you don't have is what you haven't given yourself permission to have or to accept</u>.

Your collection of voices makes up your belief system, your assumptive matrix, your world view. All of these voices, taken together, tell you what is real, how you think reality works, what is possible, what is impossible, what is thinkable, and what is unthinkable. Those voices are your programming and have been guiding your life for years. <u>They have become self-fulfilling prophecies; your assumptions about how the world works creates the world you experience</u>. So what you have made of your life to this point is a manifestation of your belief system. You have what you think it's possible for you to have. And perhaps you say that you don't want much of what you have. You say you want what you don't have, and you desire what you fear you can't have or don't deserve. But what you have is what you want. You simply are unaware of your unconscious desire, your unconscious intention, which has created what you have.

Means and Ends

You may want to resist the truth of these propositions, but your desire to resist them doesn't alter the fact that they are universal principles. If you believed it was possible to have something more, or better, or different, you would have it. You wouldn't desire it. The question is, how conscious are you of how you create what you have? Most of us think there is a distinction between means and ends. You think there is a difference between how you accomplish something and what you actually accomplish. You believe that getting what you want is largely a matter of finding the right way to get it. This belief in the distinction between means and ends is an illusion. How you live your life, is your life. How you do what you do, is what you do.

Another way of embracing this point is to accept that there is no distinction between intention and result. Your intention is evident in what you have. The material manifestation of your intention is your result. You are your results. <u>So if you want to know what your intentions are, look to the results you have produced</u>.

There are a variety of ways, an infinite number of means, to realize your intentions. At times you may confuse your method and your intention. It is your intention, not the method, that produced the result. The method is only a way your intention expresses itself. What you <u>do</u> and what you <u>have</u> is an expression of your human <u>beingness</u>. How you live your life is who you are. Your beingness expresses itself in the ways you produce results. And the clearer you are about your intention, about the purpose of your beingness, the easier it is to find ways to produce fulfilling results naturally.

Being

Consider the diagram below.

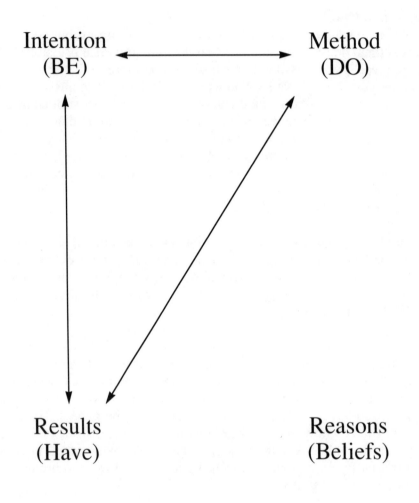

Notice that going to the reasons for your results and the methods of their production are now secondary, if not irrelevant, concerns. You can simply ask yourself if it is true for you that your results are a perfect mirror for your intention. If not, get clear about your intention. Love or your intuitive Higher Self knows what it is you really want. Listen to it and trust it. When your beingness expresses your intention, you'll have what you want. The reasons won't make any difference and the methods will become evident.

There are an indefinite number of ways to get to New York, once your intention is clear that being in New York, rather than getting to New York, is what you want. If what you want is to be getting to New York, you'll have what you want and you'll be in the process of getting there rather than actually being there. Being is more powerful than doing and having. If you want to know what your intention is, what your purpose is, what you are committed to, simply look at what you've created in your life and be accountable for your results.

When you are clear about your beingness, about your intention, about your commitment, and about the purpose of your life, what you do follows naturally. For example, if what you want is to be with people in a relationship of service, there are a variety of ways you can realize that intention. In fact, anything you do becomes a natural expression of that intention. Your results are evidence of your intention. Your results affirm your beingness. It's a positive-loop, self-fulfilling prophecy.

Your stand in life, the purpose of your life, is your willingness to be who you are. Whatever you do expresses your beingness. It all works in integrity. You have little need for reasons and beliefs to justify the rightness and certainty of your actions. Reasons aren't results. Reasons don't make methods work.

Beliefs and Reasons

Consider the diagram below.

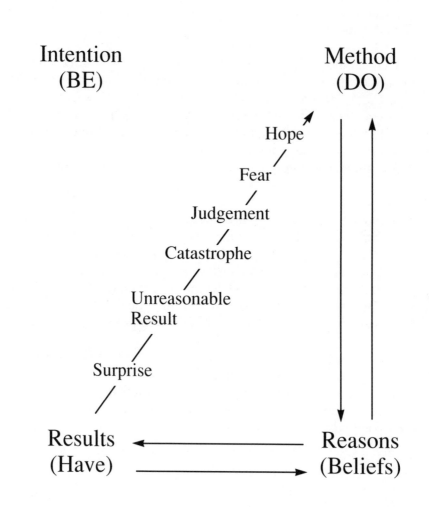

If you think you are what you have, then you have what you have because of your reasons or beliefs. Those reasons and beliefs motivate what you do. You believe that what you do produces the results you have. Sometimes the results you produce are not the results you think you want. Your reasonableness and your belief system predicted other results. At that point, you may define the outcome as an accident, or as someone else's fault, and begin to look for someone or something to blame. You look for a cause outside yourself.

When you experience an unwanted result you are surprised and feel victimized. If you assume your job as a human being is to be in control of the results you produce, then producing results over which you have no control creates a problem. You make a judgment about the results. The judgment is often that the results are a catastrophe. Your wife wasn't supposed to die. You weren't supposed to get cancer. Your business wasn't supposed to fail. You weren't supposed to be divorced. You weren't supposed to get rich. And the judgment that the unexpected result is a catastrophe actually promotes your fear of the unknown. If the surprise is evidence of the fact that you are out of control, then the illusion of control is gone and you become afraid that conditions could get worse. There could be even more catastrophes. Instead of being right about your beliefs, you're afraid that you're wrong. And being wrong questions the foundations of your identity. It questions how you think the world works.

Usually, rather than giving up your belief system, you hope instead. You hope that if you do something, things will get better. So you find yourself back at the choice to do something, something reasonable, something based on your belief system. And the reasonable activity you choose to do oftentimes produces, once again, unexpected, unreasonable results. And the loop is triggered again and again. Notice that infrequently, if ever, do you get out of the loop long enough to notice that you're out of touch with your intention and your beingness. You put your faith in your belief system and the reasons you use to assert your rightness in any situation. And being right becomes increasingly important the more often your actions produce unexpected results. You become more addicted to being right and less curious about who you are and other possibilities for doing.

Your stockpile of reasons to answer the question, "why don't I have what I want?" is endless. For example, let's say what you want is a fulfilling and satisfying career. The results you've produced, however, are largely dissatisfaction and disappointment in what you do for a living. You may believe that the reason you haven't produced the results you want is because you don't know how, you went about it the wrong way.

You may actually believe that the reason you're experiencing disappointment and lack of fulfillment is because your boss is unsympathetic, you don't make enough money, you have too little or too much training. And those reasons point to the ways you've chosen to realize your results rather than to the lack of clarity you have about your intention and about who you are. The truth is that you want the pain and frustration of failure more than the joy and satisfaction of success which could be yours if you were to get clear about your intention. You want to be right about your belief that you are undeserving of success and fulfillment, more than you want success and fulfillment.

Embracing Your Results

There's nothing wrong with being right about your beliefs and reasons, unless you want to produce different results. And if that's the case, then accept the truth that your results tell you what your intention has been. And if your results are dissatisfaction and unfulfillment, you have an opportunity to look at your intention which created your results. What's your payoff for producing dissatisfaction and lack of fulfillment? What would it cost you to change your results? You might get to be wrong about who you think you are and about how you think things work in the world. You may get to be wrong about your belief systems and your reasons for why you think things work the way they do. You may actually get to transform how it is you experience your life. That's the cost of shifting from how you run your life right now to running it in a way that creates more possibility and opportunity.

The first step is to look clearly and directly at your life and the results you've created. Next, accept the truth about how these results were produced. You're accountable for everything in your life. You are the context of your life. You don't get to be a victim of life. Even though you may not understand how you created the results you created, the truth is that you created them. They didn't just happen to you magically. You actually created what's in your life. And you get to accept all the implications of that fact, both the good news and the bad news. You don't get to accept some and reject the rest. You get to be accountable for all of it.

You get to be curious about how you created these results. Why would you want the results that you have created in your life? What's been the payoff to continue to operate out of your belief system which produces results that you say you don't want? The payoff is that you get to be right. You learned as a little child that to be right is about the most important thing in life. As nations, we fight wars and commit murder on a mass scale to be right. As individuals, we destroy relationships and beat our spouses and children to be right. We would rather be right than have lives that work productively and creatively.

So the place to begin is to look at your life and accept it as your creation. But to win at living your life, you first must surrender. To win the possibility of fulfillment, you must surrender your belief system and all your reasons for being right. <u>You must lose your life to find your life</u>. Not until then will you fully experience the truth that living life isn't about being right and being wrong. It's not even about winning and losing. It's about experiencing the Truth. It's about becoming fulfilled and fulfilling human beings. It's about developing mastery over your life.

Let's take another example. Let's say at some point in your life you made a decision to have a healthy and happy life. And as a result of living a healthy, happy life, you expected certain results. Now suppose you discover that you have cancer. If you choose to look at cancer as an unexpected, unreasonable result, and a surprise, you may experience having cancer as a catastrophe. The next likely step in the cycle is to judge the catastrophic fact of your cancer negatively. This wasn't supposed to happen. A healthy, happy life wasn't supposed to mean cancer. So you become afraid. And your fear becomes overwhelming. To save yourself from sinking into the despair and depression to which fear leads, you begin to hope. You hope that if you do something, you'll be able to change the results that surprised you. And so you do something based on your belief system, something reasonable. The reasonableness of what you do will probably not change what you have without a transformation of who you are, of your intention, of your human beingness. You feel justified in hoping because your hope is based on your reasonableness. You hope that the doctors will save you. You hope that modern medicine will find a cure before cancer takes your life. You hope that a god somewhere outside of you will save you, so you begin to pray. But without a transformation of who you are, without being willing to give up the anchored position of your belief system and your righteousness, you will continue to loop around the cycle in the hope that doing something different that will change the results. You're stuck. You're addicted to your beliefs and your reasonableness. And you're doomed. <u>There is no hope</u>.

Now let's transform the scenario. Assume that you are willing to consider the possibility that at some level beyond your conscious awareness you really did want to develop cancer. At first it sounds absolutely crazy, given the anchored position of your reasonableness and your righteousness. You now embrace the fact that you have cancer so you can experience life in a way fundamentally different from the way you had expected. You now see that having cancer is something you wanted to happen in your life for some set of reasons you have yet to discover.

I am not suggesting some simple minded "look on the bright side" thinking. I am not advocating a positive mental attitude or a Pollyanna perspective. I am suggesting a transformation, an actual shift in how you experience the conditions of your life. Such a transformation produces two things. First, you are no longer a victim of uncontrollable circumstances. Second, you are now experiencing something that you want to experience, or at least are willing to experience. Being curious about the results in your life, you now can return to examine your intention in a larger context. In that context it is possible for your experience to expand dramatically. You might decide you don't want to have cancer, that you want to live. And there is something you can do about it, and <u>you decide to heal yourself</u>. Or you may decide that you want to have cancer and what you can do is live fully and completely in every moment, including the painful ones. Those are profound realizations! You now have the power to act and to transform the present course of your life.

THE PROCESS OF CREATION

I create my reality.

I am in the process.

I embrace the process.

*As I own my power, what I
create is something wonderful.*

I create only Love.

I love my creation.

<u>You cannot have an experience in which you have not chosen to participate</u>. And you have the power to create the meaning of your experience. Experience is simply experience. It is the individual who creates and gives meaning to experience. And experience can mean whatever you want it to mean. Understanding these principles can transform your life in ways you might never have imagined possible. To illustrate, consider the following course of events. In the early 1970's, a physician by the name of Carl Simonton became frustrated when many of his patients redeveloped malignant tumors which had been previously eliminated with radiation therapy. Since radiation therapy wasn't working, he embraced his responsibility as a physician to find a way to save their lives. He was willing to look at radically different possibilities and be wrong about his present beliefs and his standards of reasonableness. He developed a visualization process in which his patients vividly and repeatedly imagined their own white blood cells seeking out and destroying the cancerous tissue in their bodies. The survival rate of his patients who performed these visualization exercises was significantly greater than it was for those patients who received only conventional treatment alone.

At the time, the medical community refused to look seriously at his findings. In the later 1970's, a psychiatrist by the name of Gerald Jampolsky, then director of the Center for Attitudinal Healing in Tiburon, California, caused the medical community to take a serious look at its assumptions, beliefs, and standards of reasonableness. He built upon what he believed most effective in Simonton's work, and counseled with thirty-six children who had been pronounced terminally ill of a variety of incurable diseases, including cancer. They had all been sent home by the medical community to die within six months or less. Several years later, every one of the children was still alive!

Jampolsky assisted each child in questioning who was in charge of their lives. He helped them realize that by being accountable for their own experience, they could alter it. He taught them to focus on the quality of life they were now living, rather than on how much time they had left to live. When the children were interviewed on the Phil Donohue Show, it was as though they had become so focused on living complete, happy, productive lives that they had forgotten about dying. They saw themselves not as victims but as co-creators of their lives in alignment with their own Creator.

It wasn't Jampolsky's work that caused the children to live. Living was merely a result. It was a function of his intention and commitment to them that promoted the recovery of their own power, their ability to act, and to create. Miracles could occur in your lives, in your homes, in your workplace, and in the world, if your beliefs would allow them to. As you come to consciousness and take responsibility for your experience of living life, anything is possible. Each of us truly is powerful in our own reality. To understand that you, and you alone, are accountable, for your experience of life allows life to take on vastly different dimensions. This realization can cause unimagined transformations to occur. You have always had the ability to create your experience. You have been doing it, both consciously and unconsciously from day one. Now it's time to expand your consciousness about your possibilities as a human being.

You intended to create the results that are your present circumstances. What's more, you want the results you've created because of the payoffs, even though in the past you have denied this.

Desire, Imagination & Focus

Now that you are clear about what your intentions have been up to this point, is there anything in your life you would like to change? If so, here's how you begin. Get a sheet of paper and write down anything and everything you would like to change in your life. When you are finished, prioritize your list. Number them in order of importance: 1, 2, 3, etc. Starting with number one ask yourself why you want this in your life. Perhaps it's a new job, or more money. Maybe it's a better relationship with your spouse, or the home you've always dreamed of owning. Whatever it is, ask yourself why you want it. If you are still absolutely clear that you want to have this in your life, ask yourself, if I had this right now, what would my experience of life be? How would I feel? What would I be thinking? What would I be doing? What would my life be like with this change? And what would it be like six months from now ? A year from now ? Are you still sure you want it? If not, repeat the process with number two. If you are sure, dig deep down inside and let your DESIRE for this change in your life magnify. Close your eyes and see your DESIRE grow. Feel how good it feels to want this. Swim around in your DESIRE. Let it envelop you. Let your DESIRE become your INTENTION. Get clear about your intention. Get COMMITTED to realizing your INTENTION.

Now IMAGINE yourself already having it. VISUALIZE what it is you want. Let your mind paint a picture of your INTENTION, your DESIRE in every detail. Experience it in its entirety! If it's a better relationship, experience all that the relationship would include. IMAGINE everything you want in the relationship; the intimacy, the loving, the forgiveness, the understanding and the acceptance.

If it is a different career, experience every detail of what you would be doing in your new line of work. Give your mind a precise picture of your intention. Once you have IMAGINATIVELY created your DESIRE in concrete detail, FOCUS on it daily.

DESIRE, IMAGINATION, FOCUS. This is the process of creation. You have been doing this to create your reality all your life. As you begin to focus on what you want, it becomes your reality. And I don't mean just dream about it. Commitment is belief in action. So act. Exercise your power. Power involves action. Action takes work. Dreaming about becoming, rather than working toward it, is just plain and simple laziness.

You now have a picture of what it is you want. Focus on it. Begin in a way that is comfortable for you. If you want to be a better parent, perhaps you can start by reading a book on being a better parent, or by listening to your child, or by spending some non-control time each day with your child. But begin. Do something about being on purpose and in alignment with your intention. As you focus your desire, your intention, what you want will begin to manifest in your physical reality.

As you work with this process, don't get discouraged. You might begin and feel good about your progress, then something in your life will come up. You will get stuck. It might be a problem at home, or some problem at work. It could be any number of things. But things do come up that can get in your way, and the next thing you know, a week or two will have passed and you'll find that you are focusing on the things you didn't want to focus on; your worries, anxieties, etc., rather than the things you want in your life. Remember, we're addicts, and addicts are scared to death of change.

Forgive yourself! This is critical. Don't go back to what doesn't work. Don't beat yourself up with your negative, self-critical voices. Focus on the voice of your Higher Self. Listen to the Love within you. Acknowledge yourself for becoming conscious of where you have been focusing your attention and redirect your focus to what it is you truly desire.

It has taken you years to get where you are. You have been programmed to do what you are doing since childhood. Change does not always come overnight. It can, but it usually takes time. Repeat the visualization process again. And realize that every time you do, you will gain more insight. See what it is you want. Each time you visualize what you want, it will become clearer. The picture will become more detailed. It will become more familiar to your whole being. Go back to your desire. Let it grow. Feel the joy and excitement of having what you want. Experience yourself realizing your desire, your intention.

To assist in the process write down on a piece of paper what it is you want. Let's say you want to lose weight. Take this piece of paper and write, "I enjoy eating less", then put it on the refrigerator. Carry another piece that says the same thing with you and re-read it at mealtimes. Create what you want. You're accountable.

The paper reads, "I enjoy eating less." By seeing this and repeating it to yourself, it will begin to sink in. If it doesn't immediately, eat. When you're done, forgive yourself. Become aware of how you feel. And go back to focusing on, "I enjoy eating less." After a time, if you continue to focus your attention on, "I enjoy eating less," you will begin to eat less.

To take this further, you might take a colored piece of paper. Let's say, pink. Cut the paper up and put a piece of it on your mirror in the bedroom. Put one in your car. Place another piece in your office. Put them everywhere you spend time. This colored piece of paper means, "I enjoy eating less!" But this way everyone else doesn't have to know about it. However, your mind knows what it means to you. Be patient. Forgive yourself. Accept yourself just as you are and realize that you are now beginning a new life, a life that will bring you what you really want. You!

THE POWER OF
COMMITMENT

I am committed to myself.

I am committed to making my life

work.

By making my life work

others will see what works.

I quietly go about doing what

works.

There was once a young man who desired wisdom. He talked with everyone about his desire and hoped that someone could tell him where he could find wisdom. One day a gentleman told him of a great master who had found wisdom and said that perhaps the young man should seek him out. So the boy decided he would. The wise man lived in a far away land and the youth had to travel for many days before he arrived. Upon entering the city where the master lived he began to inquire as to his whereabouts. He was told that the wise man could be found in a small dwelling near the sea. When the boy came to the house, the master was sitting outside relaxing in the sun. The boy felt a great excitement well up inside of him. Perhaps at last he would find the wisdom for which he had been searching.

As he approached, the old gentleman looked up and said, "I've been waiting for you, young man. Come, let's walk together." As they walked, the master asked what he could do for the boy. He quickly answered that he desired wisdom. The master said quietly, "Come with me to the sea and I will show you wisdom". The young man's heart was racing. Finally, he was sure, his search was over.

Upon reaching the shoreline the master took the youth by the arm and walked with him out into the water. When the water reached to their waists the old man suddenly grabbed the boy by his hair and pushed his head under the water. The young man began thrashing about, trying to get a breath of air, but to no avail. The old man was far too strong and agile and continued to hold his head under the water until his struggling had ceased. The master then carried the boy back to the beach and after having restored his breathing, left him lying unconscious.

When the boy awoke he was enraged. What had this stupid old man done? He had almost killed him. The boy jumped up and ran back to the old man's house, screaming, "Why did you do that to me?" The wise and loving master simply smiled and said, "When you desire wisdom as much as you desired a breath of air as I held your head under the water, you will find it!"

Perhaps many of you have heard this story told in various forms, but its lesson is timeless. It demonstrates the power of commitment. The boy gave a great deal of lip service to his supposed desire for wisdom. Perhaps he did so because he found that others paid attention to him. And I'm sure he derived many other payoffs from "searching" for wisdom. But the master finally helped him see where his commitment was. The young man was committed to "searching" for wisdom rather than "having" wisdom. He was also committed to breathing. If the boy had died, an

autopsy would have proven his commitment to breathing. His lungs
would have been full of water, thus proving the results of his commitment
to breathing. Results always demonstrate your commitment or intention.
If you would like to see what you are committed to, take a look at the life
you have created for yourself. <u>Your results will never lie to you</u>. They
will always show you what your real commitments are rather than what
you say they are. You and you alone are responsible for your life and
present situation. The life you have created for yourself is the direct result
of your commitment.

<u>Commitment is belief in action</u>! It is the cause or force within each of
us that produces results. We are all committed human beings. We are just
committed to different things. If you say you want something more,
better or greater out of life, you can have it if you choose to. So knowing
that commitment is belief in action, if your life isn't what you would
prefer it to be, you must realize that it is the beliefs you are committed to
that need to be changed. That's where the problem and confusion lie, not
in your level of commitment.

Let's say that you have problems in your relationships. You are scared
to death that your lover isn't the right person for you, or that your
companion doesn't really love you. If you believe that he/she isn't right
for you, to what are you committed? Certainly not a loving, sharing
relationship, but rather a relationship that isn't quite right. And you will
be committed to making it not quite right. The problems you experience,
your results, demonstrate your commitment to your beliefs. So until you
get your beliefs straightened out, you will continue to find relationships
that don't work. Ninety-nine percent of the time it isn't that they couldn't
work. It is simply that you are committed to having relationships that
don't work. The more relationships you have that don't work, the more
evidence you get to have to support your belief systems about
relationships. And you get to be right about your beliefs. What you don't
get is a satisfying, fulfilling relationship with a human being you love.

Another thing that happens when you get into such a relationship is
that the other person picks up on your commitment, either consciously or
unconsciously, and they pull back. They sense, consciously or
unconsciously, that you are committed to causing relationships to fail, and
it frightens them. So you have two people in a relationship working from
a place of fear, rather than one of love. Good luck in the relationship!

Or perhaps you have a weight problem and after having gone on 250
different diets you are still overweight. To what do you think you are
committed? Being thin or being overweight? And how many times have

you heard yourself say, "I just can't lose any weight?" Well guess what you have just reinforced in your mind, your bio computer? That you can't lose weight, so you don't. And there are payoffs for being overweight. Perhaps you have beliefs that you are unlovable, unwanted, or inferior. Or maybe you think that you are just not good at relationships. So to be right about your beliefs, what do you do? You walk around weighing 300 pounds to ensure that no one will love you. And you get to be right about your beliefs once again.

If you want to lose weight, I guarantee that you can, because I have done it. I have seen many people do so. All you have to do is get committed to doing it. But if you need some direction, as we all do at times, I would recommend that you purchase a book by Dr. Robert M. Giller and Kathy Matthews called <u>Medical Makeover</u>, and do what it tells you to do. It was a great help to me.

Let's use another example. Let's say that you never seem to have enough money to do the things you have always wanted to do. You have always said that you wanted to drive a Mercedes Benz, or live in a big house on the beach. But you are living in poverty in a tiny apartment, and are driving a Volkswagen bug. What are your results telling you about your commitment and beliefs? You are committed to poverty, not prosperity. You are committed to living from survival rather than abundance. And you may have hundreds of beliefs that reinforce your situation. Beliefs like:

"People with money are crooks, and I refuse to be dishonest."
"I'm just not lucky or intelligent enough to ever have a lot of money."
"I screwed up when I was younger and never got the education to do what I wanted to do with my life."
"I married far too young and now I have four children to care for and an alcoholic husband. It's just too late for me."
And so on, and so on.

If you think it's too late for you, then it's going to be too late. But don't you see that you can have anything you want because you already have it. Your power to create is immeasurable. It's just that you have been unaware that you were the one creating the results in your life. And now you are so addicted to doing what you know how to do, what you are accustomed to doing, that you are afraid to change things. Like any junkie, if someone tries to take away your stuff, you get angry. "Don't tell me I created my poverty. It was my parents' fault." "It's my wife's or husband's fault." "It's these damn kids always wanting more. It is certainly not my fault." So your life gets to be someone else's fault and therefore not your responsibility. And you get to be right, but by doing so you are placing responsibility for your life in the hands of someone else and giving away your power, which is your ability to act and change your life, if you choose to do so.

Let me clarify here that simply because you are not conscious of all your beliefs does not mean that they are not there. Much of our programming has become automatic. <u>We don't act, we react</u>. We are all committed to beliefs which create our results. And the trap we fall into is that we begin to believe that that's just the way we are and there is nothing we can do about it.

Let me share a story that demonstrates the power of commitment:

When Susan went to her kitchen one cold, stormy morning to make breakfast for herself and her three-year old daughter, Amanda, she found the child lying on the floor, semi-conscious. Amanda had been playing in the kitchen, unbeknownst to her mother. An empty prescription bottle lying beside the child told the rest of the story.

Susan quickly read the label, which said that death could occur within half an hour after loss of consciousness due to overdosage. Susan, dressed only in a small negligee, clutched the empty bottle, scooped the child into her arms and ran to the car.

The car wouldn't start. She ran back to the house to call for help. The phone was dead. Local service had been disrupted by a fallen tree.

Susan ran back to the car, grabbed her unconscious child and ran for the nearby freeway. Dressed in next to nothing, her hair still in curlers, completely unconcerned by the cold or her appearance, she scaled the fence and ran to the median strip. After laying the child down, she stepped into the oncoming traffic to stop a car. A few minutes later Amanda was in a nearby hospital emergency room. Her life was saved.

When asked later what she would have done if no one had stopped to help her, Susan said, "I would have undressed and laid naked on the freeway until someone stopped. I would have done whatever was necessary to get my child to the hospital. The moment I read the label, I saw myself in the emergency room of the hospital with Amanda. It never crossed my mind that I couldn't make it to the hospital in time. I didn't think about anything else, but getting there. I did what I had to do. I did what was necessary."

The power of commitment is the power that produces the results you want, no matter what! This power cannot be seen by the naked eye, but it can be observed in the lives of committed human beings.

Today, right now, commit yourself to yourself. Commit to do whatever it takes to make your relationships work. Commit to do whatever it takes to make your career work. Commit to do whatever it takes to make your life work. Until you are committed one hundred percent to yourself, you will never be able to commit one hundred percent to anyone or anything else. Your life can work! You simply have to become committed to doing what works. Whatever it takes and whatever it might look like in the end, you can achieve it if you get committed to its creation. Commit yourself to yourself and to doing what you know would be in your own best interest in every aspect of your life, and watch the magic happen.

LIVING FROM YOUR VISION

I have a Vision.

As I live from my Vision

my

world is transformed

into

Paradise.

Love and beauty surround me,

all else is an illusion.

Martin Luther King, Jr. had a Vision. He once eloquently spoke to over half a million people from the steps of the Lincoln Memorial and he told them, "I have a dream!" He dreamed that one day all men, black and white, could live together as brothers and sisters in peace and harmony. He had a dream of an America where there was no racial discrimination. He had a dream that some day all men could live together in Love. Martin Luther King, Jr. lived from his Vision.

But I often think how difficult it must have been for him to live from his Vision when the evidence surrounding him was screaming out another reality. As he marched in Alabama and the police turned their dogs loose on the crowds and those dogs began to mutilate the very people he had enrolled in his Vision, think of how he must have felt. The fear and the pain must have been devastating. But on he marched. He lived from his Vision and paid no attention to the ever-increasing evidence that was all around him, attempting to destroy his Vision, his Dream.

Today America is a very different place because of one man's Vision. And Martin Luther King, Jr. lives in the hearts and minds of people all over the world through his Vision.

Mohandis K. Gandhi had a Vision. He saw an India free from the tyranny of an oppressive foreign power--the British government. He lived from his Vision and after years of struggle and imprisonment the evidence came into alignment and rose to become his Vision. The British government left India peacefully. Through his Vision the life and influence of Mohandis K. Gandhi is still being felt throughout the world. His Vision and work became the inspiration for Martin Luther King, as well as many others throughout the world who are practicing Non-Violent Resistance.

Jesus Christ had a Vision. He too dreamed of a world of peace and Love where all men could live together as One. As they drove the nails through his hands and feet, by living from his Vision, He found the strength within to cry out, "Forgive them, Father, for they know not what they do." Has there ever been a greater manifestation of Love than this?

All three of these men paid the ultimate price for living from their Vision. They knew in their hearts that they were living the Truth. They knew that their Visions were Visions of Love. And by being committed to their Vision they began to transform the world and that transformation continues to this day.

My Vision

I too have a Vision. <u>I am committed to creating a world of peace and harmony within myself and in the lives of others</u>. I know that I am a loving and sensitive man and that with Love all things are possible.

There have been times when I have had smaller visions. They were visions created by my ego self. I lived in those visions and what I envisioned came to pass. But because the vision was created by my ego in its fear and its finite knowing, I found no satisfaction in the end. These visions were always much smaller than I. One must live from a Vision that is greater than one's self. One must live from the Vision given by one's Higher Self through Love. When Love, or your Higher Self, gives you a Vision and your entire life becomes committed to being about that Vision, the evidence will rise to meet the Vision. Your life and the lives of those around you will be transformed once you are <u>committed to living from your Vision</u>.

At times the evidence which is out to destroy your Vision can become overwhelming. Fear is out to create evidence to dissuade you from bringing about your Vision in any way possible. Because fear knows that once you are <u>being</u> about living from your Vision of Love there will be no more room for fear in your life. There will be no more room for fear in the world. And fear is deathly afraid of that possibility.

Love would have you become all that you were meant to become, all that you can become. Fear would have you become enslaved to it. Love desires and is committed to making your life work. Fear wants you to fail and become miserable. Your negative ego was created in fear. But it simply wants to be loved. As it experiences more Love, it will be transformed and once again become aligned with Love.

Transformation

Our Spirits create electro-magnetic fields of energy which surround our bodies. These energy fields, like all energy fields, have poles. This polarization has been centered in fear for ages. But as one begins to allow Love to flow more freely through this energy field, the poles begin to shift. As our trust in fear subsides and we begin once again to place our trust in Love, the shift will be complete and our Spirits and egos will be companions polarized in Love. The Higher Self, the Christ within you, will then become manifest. As enough people begin to experience this shift in consciousness, the entire world will be affected. But transformation begins with you, as an individual.

Trust in yourself. Trust in the inner voice of your Higher Self, which is Love. In Truth, love Yourself. Then put the messages you receive from your Higher Self into action and the God within you will emerge. Your ego, your secondary identity, will transform and will marry itself to your Spirit, which is your primary identity, and together they will bring about a state of paradise in your life. Once the world has enough people who have made this transition, the Earth itself and all the people in it will be transformed. We shall then be One in Love with all of Creation. For a thousand years we will live together, learn together and love together. What we will create will be something Wonderful which will spread throughout the Universe... Worlds without end.

Creating a Vision

What is your Vision? What are you willing to commit your life to? Create a Vision! Perhaps it's a Vision concerned with world peace and harmony, like mine. Perhaps it's about creating a world filled with Love. Close your eyes and search your hearts. Create a Vision! Live from that Vision! Work with it and listen to the words Love speaks to you. Love will share your Vision with you.

Create a contract with yourself. <u>Create an agreement with yourself that you will live from your Vision, and commit yourself to living your contract with yourself</u>. Be about your Vision. Be committed to your Vision. Be committed to yourself and be about becoming the God that you were destined to become. In every activity in which you engage, be about your Vision. When the pain, the suffering and the fear are right in front of you, live from your Vision and embrace the pain. Embrace the suffering. Embrace the fear and go through it. Don't look at the evidence. The evidence that you are not enough to bring about your Vision will be overwhelming. If you focus on the evidence, your Vision will fall to the level of the evidence. <u>Always focus on your Vision</u>.

Create a Vision about your career. Be involved in a career of creation. If it's creating a more beautiful world as a gardener or a janitor, create the most beautiful world you possibly can. Whatever that career may be, be about excellence in your chosen career. And choose a career that you love. Then love it and be all that you can possibly be in your career.

Know that what you have is what you want. Know that what you want is what you have. If you choose to have something more, embrace your desire; create a Vision of your desire and bring your Vision to pass.

Create a Vision about your relationships. Get clear about every detail you want in your relationships. See that what you really want is peace and harmony in your life and relationships. Create a Vision, live from the

Vision, and transform your reality. Once you are clear about your Vision and your Vision is in alignment with Love, the evidence will come into alignment with your Vision. You will attract all that you need for your growth to Higher Consciousness as your field of Spiritual Loving energy expands, increases, and strengthens around you. You can have it all if you so choose.

Career and relationships. Isn't that what life is all about? Creative work and loving relationships are enough. <u>Be</u> who you are. <u>Do</u> what you love. And what you will <u>Have</u> as a natural consequence will be enough. The world will be transformed through your transformation. <u>Be about your Vision!</u> <u>Live from your Vision!</u>

Barry A. Ellsworth and friends, conduct a variety of experiential workshops and trainings. These trainings are structured to give individuals and organizations an expanded, broader experience of themselves and offer them an opportunity to become aware of the possibilities in their lives. These trainings are as short as a day and as long as five days depending on your individual needs. All of the trainings are designed to facilitate "breakthroughs" in one's life or organization.

Life is a process. Discovering the process and how it works, then learning to stay in the process, lays the groundwork for miracles to occur in all aspects of life.

The workshops cover such topics as relationships, communication, sexuality, marriage, career, money, and organizational development. Besides helping you discover who you really are, the workshops will help you learn to accept and appreciate yourself more fully.

All of the trainings and workshops have but one goal:

TO MAKE YOUR LIFE WORK!

For more information on trainings, workshops or speaking engagements, write or phone:

Breakthrough
6670 Royal Harvest Way Suite 30
Salt Lake City, Utah 84121
(801) 944-0371
(801) 649-4795

To order additional copies of

Living in Love with Yourself

Please send check or money order for $8.95 plus $2.00 postage and
handling to

Breakthrough Publishing
469 Joye St.
Salt Lake City, UT 84107